Love Letters from Mount Rushmore

March 28-1940

Hello- darling — Just recieved your telegram, its surely great of Borglum to
have a car for me - It was 6:40 and
on the train flying onwards to Chicago.
Miss you very much darling and
also my dear sons. This morning train
was a pain, it stop about 6 to 8 times
but what can one do but wait and
like it - The country sides were
filled with snow, now all around
one see earth swollen with water
dirty and sad - yes waiting like
I am for life new life spring, oh!
did I eat the sandwiches, well I
surely did and how, I am riding
like the wolf - alone ate alone, read
alone, think alone - How did you
make out - were the road O.K. or
did you wait. Did you talk to Dr
Dublin? Well darling be sure and keep
in touch with me, Ill be having a
job for you soon. Well we again miss
(Aida) will be at Cleveland April 8
Martinelli sings in 2, Metropolitan opera
give 8 operas. Arrived at Chicago 10.30
train - for North western + all is well
a bit tired - Keep well, love to you
and the children Arthur
say hello to everyone for me

THE STORY OF A MARRIAGE,

A MONUMENT, AND A MOMENT

IN HISTORY   **Richard Cerasani**

Love Letters

from Mount Rushmore

SOUTH DAKOTA STATE HISTORICAL SOCIETY PRESS   *Pierre*

Picture credits: All illustrations in this book are from the
collection of Richard Cerasani unless otherwise indicated.
Restoration work on the photographs was done by Glen
Marsh Photography Studio.
Page i: image by Glen Marsh
Front cover: image by Chad Coppess. South Dakota
Department of Tourism

The paper in this book meets the guidelines for permanence
and durability of the Committee on Production Guidelines
for Book Longevity of the Council on Library Resources.

Text and cover design by Rich Hendel
Please visit our web site at www.sdshspress.com.

Printed in China

18 17 16 15 14   1 2 3 4 5

Library of Congress Cataloging-in-Publication data
Cerasani, Richard, 1938-
Love letters from Mount Rushmore : the story of a marriage,
a monument, and a moment in history / by Richard Cerasani.
    pages cm
ISBN 978-0-9860355-7-9 (alk. paper)
1. Cerasani, Arthur J., 1908-1970. 2. Sculptors—
United States—Biography. 3. Mount Rushmore National
Memorial (S.D.) 4. Borglum, Gutzon, 1867-1941—Friends
and associates. 5. Cerasani, Arthur J., 1908-1970—
Correspondence. 6. Cerasani, Mary G., 1910-2004.
7. Sculptors' spouses—United States—Biography.
8. Cerasani, Mary G., 1910-2004—Correspondence. I. Title.
NB237.C4245C47 2014
730.92'2—dc23
[B]
2013047613

*When I first started this book,
Arthur and Mary Cerasani were
simply my parents. However, the
trunk in the attic revealed a more
complete—and complex—picture
of the life they had lived for their
children and others.*

*The revelations transformed my parents
into so much more, which is why I dedicate
this book to them.*

*Thank you, Mom and Dad, for being
my true heroes.*

Contents

Acknowledgments

ords cannot fully express my gratitude to all the talented people who have helped to make this book possible, but I will try.

A world of thanks goes to: Glen Marsh, whose photographic prowess brought to life the photographs that capture the amazing story told in this book; Kathleen Kelly, whose writing talent helped to give life to my thoughts and gave shape to the hundreds of love letters hidden away for so many years; Kathleen Caine, my beautiful and devoted wife, for her patient support, insights, and gifted work on my manuscript; Rita Cerasani, my dear sister-in-law, for her special help with typing and reviewing pages and pages of manuscript; Victoria T. de Vries, whose fine editorial work helped to polish my manuscript further; and Wayne Hoffman, Sheiva Nader, Leah Lamos, Krupal Prabhker, and Roxanne Marsh, for putting their indispensable administrative and typing skills to such good use on this book project. My thanks also go to Zane Martin, Museum Specialist for the National Park Service at Mount Rushmore, and Reid Riner of the Minnilusa Historical Association at the Journey Museum in Rapid City. And finally, special appreciation goes to my literary agent Joel Tucciarone of Diadem Partners for believing in my dream of the love letters.

Black Hills

• Rapid City

Hill City

○ Keystone

Mount
Rushmore

• Hermosa

South Dakota

Black Hills

Wyoming

Nebraska

his story begins with my discovery of a trunk in the Cerasani family attic on a cold, damp autumn day in 2005. Mother, who had passed away a month short of her ninety-fourth birthday the year before, had been a schoolteacher her entire life. Her first love, after her family, was traveling the world over and learning about other countries and their cultures. Bringing something of those travel experiences home to teach her family and others was part of her routine. She had designated the attic as her own private depot, where she could accumulate these treasures.

Included among her travels were two assignments with President John F. Kennedy's Peace Corps. The first had taken place when she was seventy years old in the jungles of southern Thailand, and the second, at age eighty, in Poland. All of her memorabilia arrived at the family's front door, and it usually fell to one of her three sons to transport it to the attic. No easy task.

The attic was visited infrequently because it was not easily accessible. One had to go up to the second floor, yank on the rope hanging from the ceiling to access the pull-down ladder stairs, and then ascend the rickety staircase. As quiet as it was cold and dark, the attic also had the usual occupants, such as spiders and silverfish. Hardly a hospitable space.

My intention on this fall day was not to visit the attic to organize my mother's belongings and decide which items should go to which family member or which items should be donated or thrown away. Instead, I was focused on checking out some intriguing information I had recently heard at a family gathering.

My mother, due to her family heritage, had been a member of the Daughters of the American Revolution (DAR). That much I had known. When I heard from a relative that she had a DAR flag among her possessions, I envisioned the flag in a shadow box on my wall alongside my American Revolution and Civil War memorabilia. Locating that flag had been my sole purpose in making the pilgrimage to the dusty attic. Or so I thought.

The attic had never had much light, and this day was no exception. Its contents had no organization, just a free style of clutter with boxes and bags all over the place. Over to one side, I caught sight of an old steamer trunk surrounded by a variety of items. The trunk just sat there, as if it were the patriarch of the attic, holding court amid the clutter.

With my curiosity piqued, I carefully made my way to the trunk, which showed typical signs of wear. Leather straps were broken, and its big metal latch was rusty. I was grateful when I gave it an exploratory probe with a screwdriver and found that the trunk was not locked. As I slowly began lifting the heavy metal cover, the trunk revealed some of its contents: wrapped bundles and shoeboxes with tape around them.

For the next couple of hours, I felt like a character in C. S. Lewis's novel *The Lion, the Witch, and the Wardrobe*. Mother's trunk had transformed into the wardrobe filled with magic and memories. Slowly, the trunk revealed its treasure trove.

Image by Glen Marsh

Among the items that caught my eye were plaster busts of four presidents—George Washington, Thomas Jefferson, Abraham Lincoln, and Teddy Roosevelt, which I found all neatly wrapped in newspaper and resting peacefully toward the bottom of the trunk. I immediately realized these castings were the ones that my father had made while working for Gutzon Borglum at Mount Rushmore.

Here was a family treasure that had lain around for decades, but I felt as if I had just struck gold. In fact, I equate the intensity of my feelings to those experienced by Howard Carter, the great English archaeologist, upon finding King Tut's tomb in the Valley of the Kings.

In the midst of all this excitement came a flashback, a memory of a defining moment from my early years. In 1948, when I was a grade-school student at Ellwanger and Barry Elementary School on Linden Street in Rochester, New York, my teacher—as I recall, her name was Miss Trimble—found out that my father was an artist and had worked on Mount Rushmore. Once she had shared this information with my classmates and stressed the significance of this "mountain of granite," my life was changed forever.

Before I realized it, Miss Trimble had commissioned me to bring my father's Mount Rushmore materials to school to share with my fellow students. I dutifully went home and put together everything I could find on the monument, which my teacher had described as the most recognizable symbol of American democracy.

My presentation for the class contained original pictures of my dad climbing over the faces of George Washington, Abraham Lincoln, Thomas Jefferson, and Teddy Roosevelt and photographs of the transport system up the mountain, which was referred to as "the bucket," along with newspaper clippings and numerous other related memorabilia. After giving the presentation, I had become an instant celebrity and had experienced the unbelievable feeling that comes when someone is suddenly thrust into the spotlight.

Suffice it to say that overnight, I had become a somebody, and perhaps even a teacher's pet, as Miss Trimble would often sit beside me at my little desk and give me easy assignments. I do not recall how long my "star status" lasted, but it came down faster than a meteor and ended in disaster.

The presentation I had prepared, with all of those wonderful pictures and newspaper clippings, mysteriously disappeared from school or somehow went missing somewhere between school and home. I felt incalculable shame and guilt over the loss and kept asking myself where they could have gone and what could have happened to them. Worse yet, what would my father say?

The unsolved disappearance had haunted me for years. To think that all of the records from my father's good work and a major portion of my family's history had been lost in a grade-school "show and tell" and that I, Dick Cerasani, was the one responsible was almost too much for me to bear. Over the years, anytime I would see a TV documentary on Mount Rushmore or read a newspaper article, especially around the Fourth of July when Mount Rushmore is traditionally featured by the media, that old wound of shame would reopen with a vengeance.

After my discovery that autumn day in 2005, I began to experience a genuine release of the guilt and shame that had accompanied me since elementary school. Visiting the trunk in the attic would become my daily pilgrimage.

The most important discovery for me was the little brown envelope marked "negatives." As I started holding the negatives up to the dim light, I could make out the image of my father climbing over the presidents' faces—up and down their noses—

using the harness. Shots of the "bucket," the studio, the Hall of Records, and much more were all there. These were some of the "show and tell" photographs I had lost in grade school. What a release from guilt!

After all these years, an eagerness was rekindled in me to learn everything I could about my father's work on Mount Rushmore back in the 1940s and about my parents' lives during that time. How had he come to be hired for such an incredible job? How had my parents endured being so far apart for such a long time?

I knew that Dad had spent six months in the Black Hills of South Dakota while Mother, with no money, had been on her own in Avon, New York, caring for an infant and a toddler. Both of my parents were now gone, but here in this trunk were hundreds of their letters and my mother's diaries; I could piece together their story.

What had taken place during their lengthy separation when he was working on the mountain? The story of that time took on life and became etched into my heart, revealing a long-lost family history to me. In an odd sort of way, I felt redeemed and wanted to share the secrets of the trunk with all who might care to step back in time.

The story of my parents offers an insider's view of the events during a specific and critical time both on and off the mountain. I invite the reader to accompany me on a journey of discovery, the unveiling of a true love story rendered like an artist's painting, except not with paint but with words. The canvas is Dad's stationery; the paintbrush, his pen. Scattered across this canvas are many of the rich, deep colors of my parents' marriage: their love, commitment, sacrifice, struggles, disappointments, and joy.

On most days, Dad wrote two letters, for his need to share the details of his daily life with Mother and to express his longing for her was so great. Without a telephone and other means of direct

communication, letters became a dominant feature of their lives. Mother responded in kind. The letters became an anchor during their lives apart.

In transcribing both my father's letters and my mother's diaries, I have striven to stay true to the originals, editing only slightly to improve readability. Missing or indecipherable words are occasionally added or suggested in brackets. All emphasis occurs in the originals. When quoting directly from historical sources, I have given the title of the work and the page number in the text. The reader will need to consult the sources at the back of the book for more thorough information on Mount Rushmore.

As you embark on the journey of reading this book, I would like to share a quotation from one of America's great authors, Pulitzer Prize-winner Horton Foote: "I don't really write to honor the past. I write to investigate, to try to figure out what happened and why it happened, knowing I'll never really know. I think all the writers that I admire have this same desire, the desire to bring order out of chaos."[1] The pages that follow are an attempt to do just that—to investigate and bring order out of what seemed chaotic. Whether or not I have succeeded, only readers can judge.

1. Quoted in "Horton Foote: The Bard of Wharton," by Gregory Bossler, *The Dramatist* 2 (1990):10. Horton Foote, who died in 2009, was the recipient of the National Medal of Arts in 2000 and the Pulitzer Prize for his play *The Young Man from Atlanta* in 1995.

1 | The Artist and the Schoolteacher

The original love story begins when Arthur Cerasani and Mary Grow meet at a picnic on the Fourth of July 1935. The setting is Long Point, a park on Conesus Lake in upstate New York. On this day, the gazebo and the picnic tables are decorated with American flags, and at dusk, a large fireworks display takes place to celebrate the birthday of our country.

Gathered together are members of the Rochester Art Club, consisting mostly of painters. A member of this group is Arthur J. Cerasani, a sculptor and a painter with a number of accomplishments to his credit, one of which is winning a national soap-sculpture contest sponsored by Procter & Gamble. His sculpture had gone "on tour" to all parts of the United States. He is currently teaching art at Rochester's Memorial Art Gallery and attempting to find commissions in his chosen field.

Another member of the group is Fran Grow. An accomplished musician and a sculptor, Fran is planning to leave for Europe on a scholarship to study piano with the world-famous Nadia Boulanger, a French composer, conductor, and teacher who taught many leading twentieth-century mu-

Arthur J. Cerasani

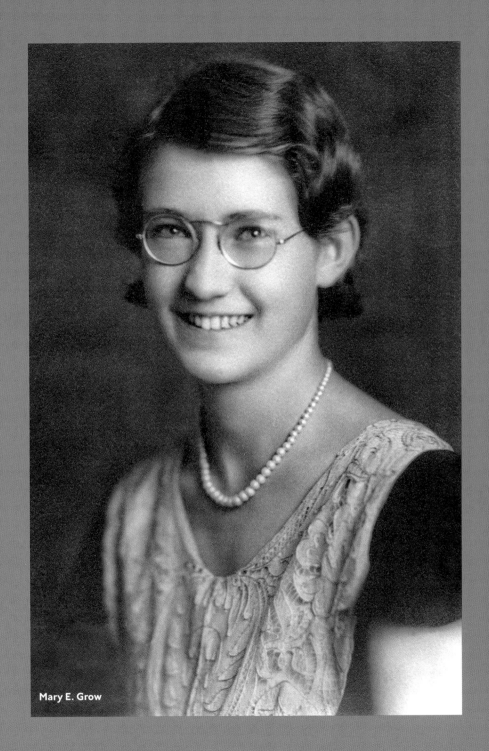

Mary E. Grow

An envelope from Mary and Arthur's courtship

sicians such as Aaron Copland. Fran has invited her sister Mary, a young elementary schoolteacher and a recent graduate of Wooster College in Ohio, to accompany her to the picnic. Mary has been fortunate to land a job as an elementary school teacher—quite an accomplishment in the middle of the Great Depression.

It would be only a matter of time before Mary and Arthur would meet at the holiday event. The rest is history. Mary Grow would later record in her diary: "We danced till 2 a.m. in the morning. . . . He is lots of fun." Early letters and postcards between my parents, Arthur and Mary, reveal a blossoming friendship and a youthful silliness. My father addressed my mother as "Dear Mother Goose and Little Red Riding Hood" and proclaimed, "My kingdom for a teacher."

By late November, their letters spoke of missing each other, and by December, love letters and poems were predominant. In early

1936, their relationship took a more serious turn. In a letter to a friend, my mother wrote: "I am engaged to Arthur Cerasani, an Italian artist, who is clever, entertaining and piles of fun. My family objects, at least Dad does."

In her diary, Mother recorded the scope of that objection:

JANUARY 22, 1936
Guess the family is a little disappointed in my engagement. Guess they think marriage with a foreign parentage won't work. Ah, North meets South—we'll make it work.

FEBRUARY 4
I heard from him saying I must believe in him, that others were trying to break our love.

FEBRUARY 12
Arthur's parents don't speak English but I don't mind.

FEBRUARY 26
Gee I think Arthur is swell. Hope nothing happens to us to keep us apart . . . families having fits about us. His family tells him to forget about me, and mine says, "Don't be in a hurry." . . . Fran says I will have 18 kids if I marry Arthur and piles of "wops" following us about.

FEBRUARY 29
I told [a friend] about our engagement. She seemed to think it's sweet. I would be engaged to an Italian but admitted that we were given wrong opinions of the Italian race because of the general type that have come to America. . . . Arthur and I danced at the coffee shop until 2 a.m.

The Cerasani family

The Grow family

Mary and Arthur Cerasani pose for
a wedding picture on July 11, 1936.

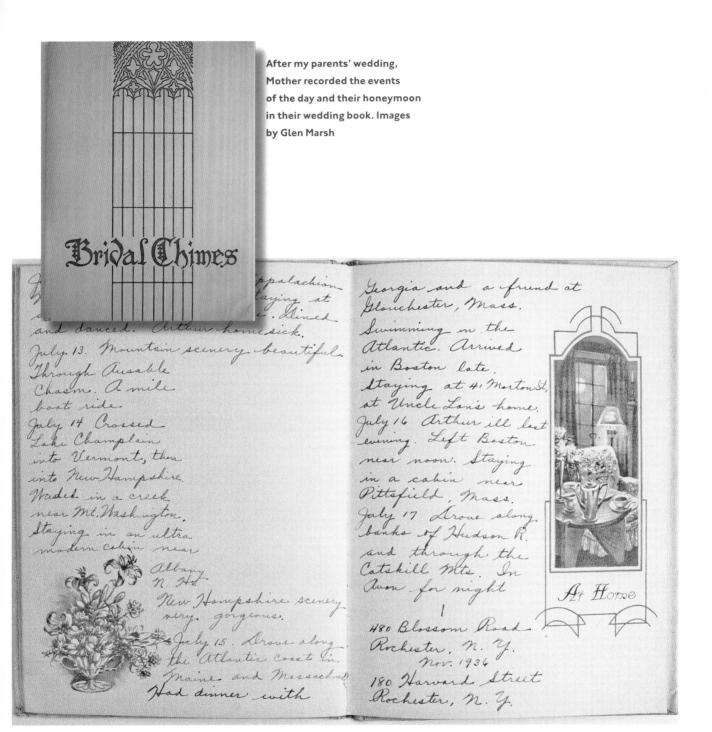

After my parents' wedding, Mother recorded the events of the day and their honeymoon in their wedding book. Images by Glen Marsh

Bridal Chimes

Appalachian ... staying at ... . Dined and danced. Arthur homesick. July 13. Mountain scenery beautiful. Through Ausable Chasm. A mile boat ride. July 14 Crossed Lake Champlain into Vermont, then into New Hampshire. Waded in a creek near Mt. Washington. Staying in an ultra modern cabin near Albany N. H. New Hampshire scenery very gorgeous. July 15. Drove along the Atlantic coast in Maine and Massachusett. Had dinner with

Georgia and a friend at Glouchester, Mass. Swimming in the Atlantic. Arrived in Boston late. Staying at 41 Morton St, at Uncle Lou's home. July 16 Arthur ill last evening. Left Boston near noon. Staying in a cabin near Pittsfield, Mass. July 17 Drove along banks of Hudson R. and through the Catskill Mts. In Avon for night

480 Blossom Road
Rochester, N. Y.
Nov. 1936
180 Harvard Street
Rochester, N. Y.

At Home

MARCH 3
Arthur, he stands a lot of nagging, which is against our being married.

MARCH 23
He realizes our families aren't much for our marrying . . . we are standing lots of opposition.

As the diary entries indicate, my father, a first-generation Italian, had some obstacles to overcome. His parents did not speak English and, like most new immigrants to this country, lived in the less desirable area of town. To use an old cliché, Dad came from "the other side of the tracks."

In contrast, my mother was a Daughter of the American Revolution. Her family, by anyone's standards, was considered rather well off. Her father, George C. Grow, had oil properties and a good place in American society. Despite the Great Depression, mother's father was doing all right. The price of a barrel of oil was often his biggest concern.

In examining all the letters and diary entries, I cannot help but note the similarities to Shakespeare's *Romeo and Juliet* or Leonard Bernstein's *West Side Story*. While I cannot claim that inequalities between the Cerasanis and the Grows were likely to explode after the manner of the Capulets and the Montagues, similar issues were present: differences in social class, related prejudices, and "stick to your own kind" mentalities.

Adding to these problems were events unfolding on the world scene during their courtship, events that did not help to ameliorate the differences between them. The Italian leader Benito Mussolini was then one of the bad boys on the world stage. His imperial aspirations became clear with his 1935 invasion of Ethiopia, and in 1939, he would formally align his country with another aggressive power, Nazi Germany. Italy and Mussolini were often in the headlines, and that was certainly not good news for Dad. Opposition intensified. Mother wrote to encourage him:

MARCH 25, 1936

Darling, . . . Of course, you will make me happy. We will make each other happy and strong and brave. It all sounds startling and maybe hard, but the hardest part is right now for we are restless and uneasy.

When we are married we shall have more confidence, and more peace of mind. Even though our path should prove to be a hard one, we will have something stable and durable to fall back upon, and to console ourselves by that great foundation — love.

Darling, I do love you very much and I want you to be happy and well. Worry destroys so much energy and vitality. In working for each other, be ready for battle. I'm ready for battle.

In spite of all the obstacles, Mom's diary recorded what happened next: "July 11, 1936, at 9:30 a.m., my name became Mrs. Arthur John Cerasani. Just the two families and the minister Charles Matthews and his wife were present. Arthur was late to his own wedding. It was to be at 9:00 A.M."

No matter where one starts in the diaries of my mother, Mary Cerasani, life, as she reported it, was tough. Whether 1937, 1938, or 1939, the country was still struggling with the effects of the Great Depression. It was not uncommon for individuals to go door to door in search of any kind of work or food to ease their hunger.

By 1939, my Dad had been out of a full-time job for six months. Wherever and however he searched, he could not find permanent employment. Teaching evening classes in casting and sculpting brought in a dollar per student per class, and whenever the required fifteen-person enrollment was not met, classes were cancelled. He looked for part-time work, hoping to make extra cash. The stockroom at a department store occasionally gave him some work. On February 1, 1937, he earned a dollar for clearing six inches of snow.

Mother's diary records the daily struggle: "Art still has only a class in casting at the Art Gallery once a week, which brings in very little to pay for living. Art's parents still supply us with food. Art's mother gave him $1.00 and my Dad gave him $5.00. This makes me very ill. I prefer doing with-

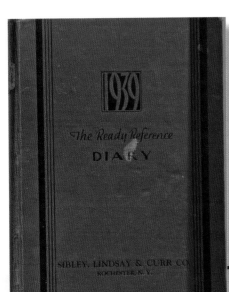

Mother's diary describes
the family's day-to-day
life in the summer of 1939.
Images by Glen Marsh

Tuesday June 6 Helen Spencer drove Arthur Jr & me to Avon at 9:30 this A.M. She had dinner at Mama's with us. It is so good to get a breath of fresh air & warm sunshine. Lately my face has looked old & my eyes dull. Dad says Arthur Jr is the most active child he ever saw in all his life - with no exception. Mrs Woolford, Art's voice teacher, says he should be free of all financial worries - someone should have gone there to back him.

Wednesday 7 This afternoon Art & I took Arthur Jr & Richard to Kodak Co. hoping sometime they will be called as models. They said they might be called soon. The babies are so darling. Arthur Jr wanted to get on every streetcar & had regular tantrums when we didn't. Over to Carasonis this evening. To bed late again.

Most of the underground tunnels in Europe are ventilated by natural drafts sweeping from one end to the other. If this method were used in the Holland or Lincoln or Queens Midtown Tunnels in New York, they would need a gale traveling 72 miles an hour to provide the necessary ventilation.

[84]

Thursday June 8 Washed clothes again today & ironed. Arthur Jr goes to toilet OK - now but stands on his nursery chair so I do have extra work with him yet. He is extremely head strong - sweet as the dickens until he is opposed & then - a regular tantrum. Over to Fangrades this P.M. To bed late as usual. My eyes & head smart plenty - from lack of sleep.

Friday 9 Clotilda & Ewel mblack went to Oakhill Country Club to the Nazareth College Dance this P.M. Art & I didn't think we could afford to go until too late to get a bid. Art over to his house all evening though he told me he would be right back when he left at 7:30 P.M.

One of the latest innovations is the invention of fireproof wood. It can be tooled and cut as well as other wood. It is made fireproof by being treated with ammonium salts.

[85]

the struggle | 23

My grandfather, Luigi Cerasani, holding my brother, Artie, stands with Dad outside of my grandparents' home.

out." Another entry lamenting that all he had earned the last two weeks was one dollar ends with, "We buy almost nothing . . . we are fast driving to the end of our resources."

The biggest expense my parents had in 1939 was the upkeep of their two children. Art Jr., born May 18, 1937, was now two years old, and I, Dick, born October 25, 1938, was one year old. Cutting back anymore to live within their means was not really possible. In spite of the joy of having children, the additional expenses weighed heavily on my parents, and they worked twice as hard to increase their income. There was no lack of willingness to work, only lack of opportunity, as Mother's diary entries reveal:

FEBRUARY 13
Art out all day casting two small objects that will only bring in $3.50. We are in bad circumstances.

FEBRUARY 14
Art sad because he didn't have money to buy me a Valentine present.

In addition to taking care of two toddlers, Mother continued to try to earn cash for the family. She knocked on doors, trying to sell all-occasion greeting cards. As it turned out, she was quite successful: "Home this evening weak and tired. In 2 ½ weeks, I did $248.00 in business—making me nearly $100.00 profit. It is work that eats the soul of a person right out, this selling or taking orders house to house." Considering those economically hard times, her sales results seem exceptional, but more often than not, our family came up far short of our needs. "We have no money not even enough to pay Sept. rent," Mother noted, "& we see no place to get it."

For an artist like my Dad, shoveling snow, fixing machinery, running errands, and doing any odd job he could had to be humiliating. Mother also recorded his struggles in her diary: "He is very hard to manage . . . wants to commit suicide. He is a man with many talents and possibilities, but also lost energies." Friends and relatives were often what kept our family going. "We have no money, not even to buy the art paper. Art's parents bring us our food," Mother wrote, adding, "We managed to finish paying our rent for this month but told the landlord we would have to leave October 1st."

SATURDAY, OCTOBER 9
My days are dreary except for the boys, and they are dears. My back and head ache almost constantly. Art is gone most of the time. He stays at Lewis Street for supper and all evening. For the time he pretends to be looking for a job, [but] he accomplishes little. It is awfully hard to exist without any money at all. We have absolutely not a penny. It is getting to be wearing.

The situation could easily be viewed as a composite snapshot of many families during the Great Depression who were forced to do whatever they had to do to survive. A week before my family was to become homeless, a solution arrived in the mail. It was a letter from Mother's father and is dated September 21:

Dear Mary,
Your letter of September 17th received. I was glad to hear from you and in regard to your coming to Avon to live with us, want you all to feel that you are welcome.
There is plenty of room, and Arthur can be there with you as much as possible.

Mertie Grow, my maternal grandmother, holds Artie, while my grandfather George Grow holds our cousin Cindy at their home.

The Grow family house as it looks today. Image by Phoebe Grow

The economic hardship made family separation necessary. Mother wrote: "Until Arthur gets a job and can support us, this will have to be." Avon, where Mother had grown up, was a small town about twenty-five miles from Rochester, New York. A mostly agricultural community with its rolling hills, little town square, and band shell, it was a great place for kids to grow up, a place where everybody knew everybody.

On October 1, Dad returned to his family's home in Rochester, the home of Eastman Kodak and a large industrial city. By living in Rochester, he would be more likely to find work, and he could visit us on weekends.

Just as my parents were adjusting to the new realities of their lives, a great sadness was about to befall them. Mother wrote in her diary:

NOVEMBER 7

Received a telegram from Boston saying operation is over, ¾ of stomach is gone. Mama resting. Letter explaining will follow.

NOVEMBER 8

Fran called from Boston saying that Mama died this a.m.

The sudden death of my maternal grandmother was a devastating blow to my mother and her closely knit family. Thanksgiving and Christmas 1939 were celebrated with a heaviness that was deeply felt by all, but Mother's diary recorded her happiness that she had at least been able to spend six weeks of meaningful time with her mother prior to her death. That was the silver lining in the cloud of mourning.

On January 2, 1940, Mother had reported some good news: "Art has had a job for about a month. He repairs machinery at the Todd Company at $19.80 per week. He is staying in Rochester during the week with his parents and spending weekends with us in Avon."

Eight days later, on January 10, 1940, an event took place that would be life-changing for Dad.

On January 10, 1940, Dad was at his parents' home located at 191 Lewis Street in Rochester, New York, when he answered a knock at the door. On the front porch stood an older man with white hair, prominent ears, and a mustache. My Dad reported the conversation in the following way.

"Hello," the stranger began, "the Rochester Memorial Art Gallery has informed me that local artists live at this address. I need some help on the casting of a bust. It will be of Frank Gannett, the owner of Gannett newspapers. Am I at the right place?"

Caught by surprise, my father told the man that he had indeed come to the correct address. "I am an artist, sir, to be precise, a sculptor and a painter. During the week, I live in Rochester and teach art."

"Good, and I am Gutzon Borglum."

Only six months before, my parents had traveled west to visit relatives in California. During the journey they had taken a detour and driven through the Black Hills of South Dakota, stopping to see the carvings of Mount Rushmore. In my mother's diary for that day, her entry reads: "Wouldn't it be nice to be working here as a sculptor on this historical undertaking."

Now, a mere six months later, who was standing on the doorstep before Dad but the famous sculptor of Mount Rushmore! My father invited him in, and Mr. Borglum explained that he needed a clay model of a bust he had been commissioned to execute. My mother recorded in her diary that night: "This evening Arthur called saying he was casting a head for the sculptor Gutzon Borglum. It is of Mr. Gannett of Rochester." Additional entries convey details of my parents' relationship with Borglum:

JANUARY 12
Found Arthur working on Frank Gannett's sculpture by Gutzon Borglum. I met Borglum. He is very charming. He wastes no time. As soon as he arrived, he went right to work helping Art with the head. He has asked Art to go out to South Dakota to work with him near the Rushmore Memorial. He said he would get more pay and advancement.

JANUARY 13
Borglum left last night for NYC telling Art to be sure to keep in touch with him; he definitely wanted him with him.

Dad never told us exactly what he was thinking at the moment he met the famous man, but to say he was surprised is most certainly an understatement. That knock at the door was the beginning of a relationship that would affect our entire family life. It would also alter the course of my father's career.

Hope finally loomed on the horizon, and the atmosphere was full of joy. The fact that the offer of work had come from a famous artist generated much energy and excitement in the Grow and Cerasani clans. Meanwhile, Dad continued doing any work that he could find while waiting for instructions from Borglum as to when to come to South Dakota. Mother's diary recorded that

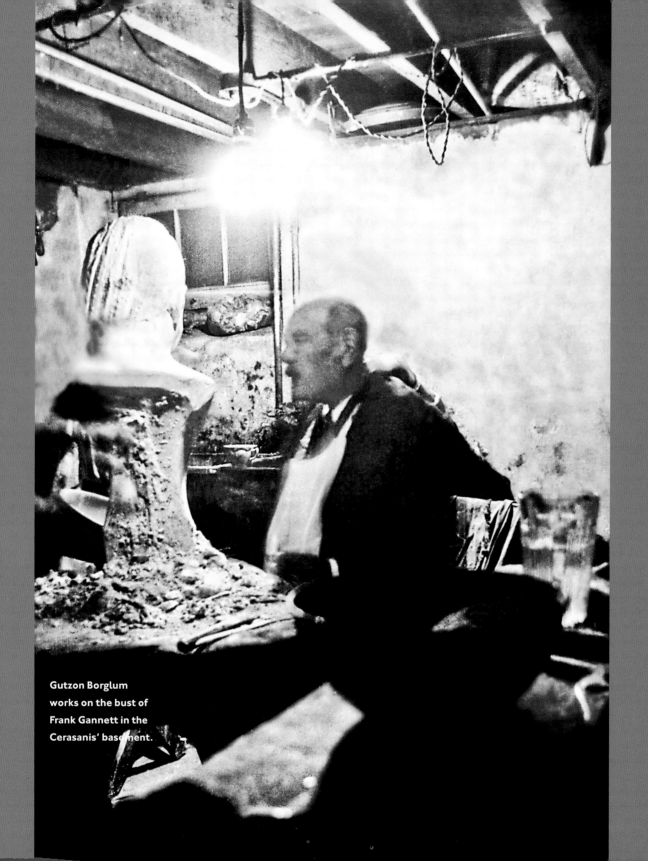

Gutzon Borglum works on the bust of Frank Gannett in the Cerasanis' basement.

 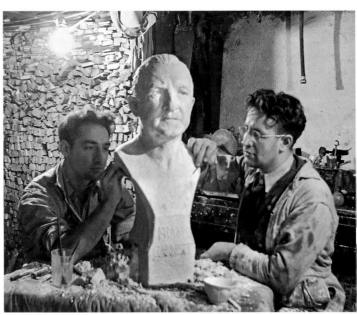

(*left*)
Mother and Dad
examining the Gannett
bust

(*right*)
Americo, Dad's brother,
works with him on the
commissioned bust.

Dad took home $1.50 for a day shift and $1.25 for an evening shift, "when he could find someone to hire him."

The long, cold winter days started to add up, and the weeks of waiting turned into a couple of months. After Dad had received neither word nor a reply after three attempts to reach Borglum, "the big break" turned into "the big wait." Mother and Dad looked forward to the mail each day but were disappointed. What was the meaning of Borglum's silence, and how long would they have to wait for some news?

Eventually, the lack of news from Gutzon Borglum had my parents doubting the sincerity of the famous sculptor's offer. Was the promise of working with him based on empty words? Was Borglum just some sort of a politician or a charismatic celebrity making a promise without any intention of following through?

Little did they know, but during this time, Gutzon Borglum was also struggling. Only later would they learn of the sculptor's

The March 20, 1940,
letter from Gutzon
Borglum asking Dad
to come and work
at Mount Rushmore

MOUNT RUSHMORE
NATIONAL MEMORIAL COMMISSION

COMMISSION	EXECUTIVE OFFICES	EXECUTIVE COMMITTEE
William McReynolds, Chairman W. J. Bulow, Vice Chairman Russell Arundel, Secretary	Mount Rushmore Keystone, South Dakota	Kent Keller, Chairman E. F. McDonald, Jr., Vice-Chairman Russell Arundel, Secretary
George W. Norris L. B. Hanna John Townsend Isabella Greenway Hart Kent Keller Lorine J. Spoonts E. F. McDonald, Jr. William Williamson George Philip		W. J. Bulow William Williamson William McReynolds, Ex-Officio

COMMITTEE ON DESIGN AND PUBLICITY

Gutzon Borglum, Sculptor-Director
Doane Robinson, Historian
Lincoln Borglum, Superintendent

Gutzon Borglum, Chairman
W. J. Bulow   George Philip
E. F. McDonald, Jr.   Lorine J. Spoonts
William McReynolds, Ex-Officio

March 20, 1940

Dear Arthur Carasoni:-

Your letters have been received--all of them I believe, and
the only reason that you have not received an answer is that I have
been in the hospital, away from home and I'm ill.

I wish that you would make your plans about the first of April,
Come two or three days before or after; it doesn't make any differ-
ence which. I have made arrangements for the work that I want you
to do. It will be work that you like to do. When you come and have
been at work a week or two, and can understand conditions here I
will talk to you about your brother if you would like to have him
come and if he wants to.

If you have a little automobile of your own you will find it
very convenient out here, but if you only have one for the family I
wouldn't advise bringing it; come by train. I want you to arrange
to live near the work on the mountain. There are many people there
and you can have plenty of company and be very comfortable.

Please write to me at once and tell me your plans.

Very sincerely yours,

Gutzon Borglum
Sculptor-Director

Mr. Arthur J. Cerasani
191 Lewis Street
Rochester, N. Y.

MOUNT RUSHMORE
NATIONAL MEMORIAL COMMISSION
EXECUTIVE OFFICES
KEYSTONE, SOUTH DAKOTA

OFFICIAL BUSINESS—FREE

Air Mail
INLAND AIR LINES

Mr. Arthur J. Cerasani
191 Lewis St.
Rochester, N. Y.

difficulties, which, for the most part, centered on health issues. Finally, two months and ten days later, on March 23, 1940, Holy Saturday, news from Gutzon Borglum finally arrived.

Family members have told me that Gutzon Borglum's long-awaited letter, written a few days earlier, precipitated an outbreak of exuberant joy. Mother was ecstatic that her husband, a talented artist, had finally received the recognition he deserved. As for Dad, I can only imagine that, with his exceptional tenor voice, he must have broken out in full vocal expression, as he was prone to do during happy times. He may have assumed the character of Rodolfo in Act One of *La Bohème*, singing, *"Che gelida manina!"* ("What a cold little hand!"). Dad loved to hit those high notes through which he could express power and great joy. After all, he had studied that role with his voice coach from the Eastman School of Music. As a child, I remember numerous times when Dad would show off those high notes in front of family and friends as a way of celebrating and expressing good news.

The celebration of Borglum's message continued that evening, with Dad taking Mother out dancing. Mother's diary states that Dad had been scheduled to sing in a minstrel show the coming week, but it had been quickly decided that a possible singing career would have to take a back seat to an actual job.

On the next day, which was Easter Sunday, Dad sent Gutzon Borglum a night letter saying that he would leave on Thursday for South Dakota. Then on March twenty-fifth, a letter arrived, this time from the executive offices in Keystone, South Dakota, confirming the need for Dad to arrive at Mount Rushmore. For the next couple of days, Mom and Dad scrambled to get him ready for the trip. A Western Union telegram arrived on March 28th, giving Dad further instructions.

4 | *Early Days in South Dakota*

Over two and a half months had passed since that knock on the door and my father's first encounter with Gutzon Borglum on the front porch of his parents' home in Rochester, New York. The prolonged silence had been broken by the letter acknowledging that Gutzon Borglum was hiring him. Now, my father was finally on his way to fulfilling his dream in what was for him the chance of a lifetime.

"Art and I drove to the New York Central Railroad Station in Rochester, this morning," Mother wrote in her diary on March 28, 1940. "There was heavy fog, making the trip difficult. We were quite calm, though our hearts were heavy because of the departure. I hope and pray that his new adventure means something good in the way of advancement for him and that I can go there soon to be with him." One can only imagine the thoughts racing through their minds as the time to say goodbye approached. They had no idea how long they would be apart, nor what would transpire in both their lives during my father's sojourn in South Dakota.

Once again they found themselves at the New York Central Railroad Station, where four years earlier their lives together had begun. Mother's bridal book entry for February 7, 1936, had read: "Arthur placed the engagement ring on my finger in the New York Central R.R. Station, Rochester, N.Y., at about midnight. I had just heard *Faust* at the Eastman Theatre." This starting place for their life-long commitment to one another had now become an ironic symbol of their separation.

Somehow, my mother found the inner strength to put my father on the train to Rapid City that day in March, knowing that he was leaving her alone with two small children to care for and that it would be a struggle for her to find the means to obtain enough money to feed and clothe the family. Many questions must have swirled around in her mind: How will Arthur do at Mount Rushmore? How long will he be away? When will I see him again? How am I going to manage without him?

In her diary, she clearly expressed her emotions: "I feel very hollow and empty just at the thought of Art being so far away." This statement was followed by something no one in the family had known. Evidently, she had not even told my father about it before his departure. "On top of all," she wrote, "I believe I'm pregnant again and physically near a nervous wreck now." One can assume that she did not tell Dad because she did not want him to stay home with her and sacrifice his dream. It is fair to say that my mother placed his happiness and need for fulfillment above her own.

Mother returned home, and Dad began his journey with anticipation and speculation as his travel companions. He spent the next two days and two nights on various trains: Rochester to Chicago and then on to Keystone with numerous stops along the way.

While he was on the train, Mother sent him a telegram giving him further instructions about his arrival. Borglum would have a car waiting at the station to pick him up. Dad's postcards writ-

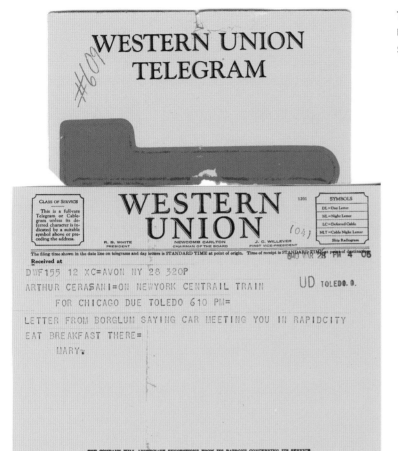

WESTERN UNION
TELEGRAM

#609

WESTERN
UNION

1201

CLASS OF SERVICE

This is a full-rate Telegram or Cable-gram unless its de-ferred character is in-dicated by a suitable symbol above or pre-ceding the address.

R. B. WHITE
PRESIDENT

NEWCOMB CARLTON
CHAIRMAN OF THE BOARD

J. C. WILLEVER
FIRST VICE-PRESIDENT

(04)

SYMBOLS

DL = Day Letter

NL = Night Letter

LC = Deferred Cable

NLT = Cable Night Letter

Ship Radiogram

The filing time shown in the date line on telegrams and day letters is STANDARD TIME at point of origin. Time of receipt is STANDARD TIME at point of destination

840 MAR 28 PM 4 05

Received at

DWF155 12 XC=AVON NY 28 320P

ARTHUR CERASANI=ON NEWYORK CENTRAIL TRAIN   UD TOLEDO. O.

FOR CHICAGO DUE TOLEDO 610 PM=

LETTER FROM BORGLUM SAYING CAR MEETING YOU IN RAPIDCITY

EAT BREAKFAST THERE=

MARY.

THE COMPANY WILL APPRECIATE SUGGESTIONS FROM ITS PATRONS CONCERNING ITS SERVICE

ten on the ride to South Dakota give some insight into his initial hopes and expectations. "It's surely great of Borglum to have a car for me," he wrote on March 28. The countryside outside the train was "waiting like I am for life, new life, spring." On arrival in Rapid City on March 30, he scribbled, "What luck!! I think I will be living by Mt. Rushmore."

Dad's enthusiasm was still evident even after the arduous days of travel. Arriving before dawn, he wrote a postcard home with the news that there was "no one at the station waiting for me but—I suppose it is [too] early for them." Here he was at 6:15

Postcards from Dad sent love and information to Mother during his journey to South Dakota.

A.M. on a dark, isolated, and presumably cold train platform with no one to greet him. To make matters worse, his travel trunk, which Mother had packed for him, was missing. Not on the train when he arrived, it most likely had been misplaced when he was making one of his connections, and for all he knew, it could have been back in Chicago.

Time passed, until the minutes grew into hours. My father must have agonized again about his decision to work with Borglum at Mount Rushmore, the enchanted mountain where an artist like himself could pursue his love for creative expression. Here, he would have the opportunity to use his hands as a sculptor instead of doing the work he had been forced to do for the last few years in order to meet his family obligations. It had to have weighed heavily on him that his wife and their two young children were forced to fend for themselves at home, while he had set off with the hope, not a guarantee, of making a better life for all of them.

The hours continued to pass without anyone coming from Borglum's operation. Then, after ten hours, a man finally showed up to drive Dad to his new job.

Dad's first letter to Mother after his arrival revealed his impressions:

Mount Rushmore
March 30, 1940
25 to 11 p.m.
My most adorable wife,
Darling if God ever made a lonesome man — one whose very heart is breaking — he made me. Never have I missed or longed for any thing or any body as I do now. Now I realize what you meant. Nature with its beauty can not replace the hunger for human life — it really is cruel its very silences hurt the ears its bigness destroys our sense of balance. What extremes are these.

My day has been so unpleasant. It started by my trunk not reaching Rapid City. Borglum thought I was coming Sunday, so no one was at the station, its cost me plenty calling so I remained at Rapid City waiting for the 3:15 train — it came but no trunk, so I [was] waiting from 6:15 a.m. to 4:15 p.m. for someone to come. They did in an old truck — driving like mad over hills and curves. Arrived no Borglum or son. The place is a mess, conditions are miserable, dirt and [filth]. And the people, the place I ate would make one [think] of the story Jr. Grow [tells] about [Mother's brother had experienced third-world conditions in the oil fields of Venezuela, where he worked as a geologist for Standard Oil]. Low ceiling, 4 beds, smoke, no place to take a

*bath — some of the fellows go to Rapid City for baths. The Gov
Agent [Frank Skells] sent me to an empty office to sleep tonight.
It's cold (no heat) so I am sleeping with bath robe. If only you
could have [seen] what I saw and the place and the people you
would not have stopped. It's no place for good people. I'll see and
have a talk with Borglum as soon as I can, now I can not return,
I will have to fight, what [breaks] my heart is the fact that as
soon as I saw conditions and the people I knew I could never see
you again — that is, not here. I could never have my wife and
children come to this, this is not progress, it's not even life. It's a*

good thing I have a picture of you smiling it gives me strength, and God I really need it here. I am writing this to you because I love you and want you to know the truth, please don't show it to anyone. So forget any plans of coming here—if I can, I'll see what else there is to this wonderful place. Most of the married people live at Keystone, 3 miles from here—but they say rents are high—living is high and the places are rotten. Forgive me if this sounds boyish but it's the truth—Goodnight sweetheart and God bless you and the children and keep you well. Write darling and be happy. I fight, see to the very end.

Love Arthur

Then, in a kind of postscript, Dad added a few extra lines:

"[T]he altitude is 5,700 where I am staying, it hurts the ears. Monday will tell what I am to do—and why. How are things at home? Just had dinner. . . . Going to Rapid City with the boys—will write tonight. Your Affectionate Hubby."

The following day's letter was not more optimistic, although one can sense a more philosophical tone. It also responded to some startling news he had just received from Mother.

Keystone, SD
March 31, 1940
My darling wife:
How are you tonight? Write and tell me about your self and the children. Are they well? Did you see the Dr? And are you really!!? Mary, I am really glad I came; it makes me realize what a lucky man I am having you. You know I love you very much to do this, you really cannot conceive what it is all about.

I shall not burden you any more with my troubles. They are things I must take and do the best I can with. Whatever I do, this experience must serve us. When I learn more about what I am to do—salary and etc. I will be in a better position to judge—and write.

Living can be crude but this place takes the cake. The people here are perfectly happy with the crudity and filth. They eat, sleep and play pool and drink. I hope I can profit by the lesson. I pray there is something in store that will make up for the miserable conditions the danger to my health and the stagnation of my finer interest in life. But it may make me wiser. I think it would be good if you wrote a letter for me to Mrs. Moore and send it so I could rewrite it, asking to be considered for Fran's job

In contrast to Keystone, Rapid City was a budding metropolis that offered entertainment, shopping, and a respite from the isolation of Mount Rushmore. Minnilusa Historical Association at The Journey Museum, Rapid City, S.Dak.

[Mary Cerasani's sister, the artist]. You see darling I had a talk with the Government agent here—he likes me and has informed me in confidence to have a heart to heart talk with Mr. Borglum, and also informed me the job may last only until June. So you see we must be careful with our plans. It is getting colder and my nose is bleeding so must close. Goodnight darling. Your affectionate Arthur . . .

Oh! Did I tell you I rode in to Rapid City this afternoon to get my trunk and had to go to a movie with the people that drove me, and guess what we saw. Castles on the Hudson—a prison picture and was it passable. And did the driver drive, what fools, just as crazy as they make them, they drive all over the road, they fly.

Don't tell any one about anything I have written.

How is this for a good boy—I have refused drinks not a one.

Hope I was home close to you sweetheart.

Missing you

Arthur

No place to take a bath no toilets, out door affairs it is sad but it is the truth.

Goodnight, my dearest love.

For all the disillusionment and disappointment he had already endured during his first week away from home, Dad's next letter would be the most startling of all. April first, better known to western civilization as April Fools' Day, was to be a crushing day for Dad's aspirations. Lincoln Borglum, substituting for his father, Gutzon, showed up to greet Dad and informed him of the work he was to do. My father recorded this meeting in a long letter to Mother later that day. Most disappointing, he told Mother, was the news that he would not be casting or sculpting; he would be surveying.

Monday evening April 1, 1940

Dear Mary,

I recieved your letter this evening. It was great to hear from you. There is little I can say as far as information goes. I have met Lincoln Borglum and have had orders what to do. And if you think they are easy - you must guess again, That is Gutzon's orders. This morning I have started to make a scale reproduction of all the grounds. It covers all the park area. type po graphical surv. a map to scale, what a problem. After this one is made we are to do a great one emense in size, poor me.

All seems a dream, a mystery here I am all alone in the new office Bld. cold. I hope they can fix a place here for me to stay. It is away from every body, No one to talk. I spent all day at the studio with an assistent. The person that is working with me is a pointer on the mountain. The casts are in the studio they are 1/20 of the real heads, about 20 inches high. There was little head there. The studio is a great big affair. We tried hard to put enough logs in the big fire place - but no use. A thick fog has swollowed the whole country side it is like a cold wet breath wetting everything. It started about 9:30 this morning. first swollowing Keystone and then taking the lower slops of the Mts. untill the heads all disappeared - leaving a heavy milk fog over everything. Our small settlement at the Mt. is called Rushmore. Keystone is about 3 miles away - and old mining town. like you see in the movies. everything is old and falling apart - people have just really started to live there since the mount

This letter from April 1, 1940, details Dad's disappointment about the work he was hired to do.

Rushmore work - it was an empty town for about 40 years. Rapid city is about 23 miles away - so you see there is little to do. We start work at 1st and quit at 4.00. giving one a long night to be lonely with. Sorry I did not bring my Fraction chart. This as I see it is going to be a big fight. but I will fight. Forgive my writing but I do all my writing in bed! Could not sleep last night so cold. I pray Borglum comes, I don't know what I am working for.

I did write. and also told you I had recieved you telegram on the train at toledo. What writting! well maybe its because I am sleepy. Oh! mama tomarrow I go up up up to the heads on the mountain for survey work. What fate - ah! it is my destiny. Gee! mama I hope I could earn enough money so we could be together again, that is not here, This is no place for you and the children, I say this sweetheart, because I love you very much.

Mama about the radio - you can fix it take that small shaft and put it back as far as you can and tie it. that should be like this ⌒ it may be like this now ⌒ tie it like this to hold it back. Just had Co. A fellow and his wife - wasted 2½ hrs. the girl is going to have a baby. and the fellow wants me to help - him in art - just found out that for food a week it's going to cost me $7 or a week and what about sleep oh! oh! Well how are things mama darling go right away to Dr Zu. you really cannot now. Take care of your self darling I love more then life - Goodnight sweet - Keep well and strong

Luv Arthur

we should all it's national love day april fools day - Ha!

Dad must have been dumbfounded as he listened to what Lincoln Borglum told him. Leaving his family to do what? Had a mistake been made here? My father had never worked as a surveyor. In Rochester, he had worked alongside Borglum as a sculptor, helping with the casting of the Frank Gannett bust, and that was what he believed he had been hired to do.

After all, Gutzon Borglum's letter of March 20 had made the Rushmore job official and seemed clear enough: "I have made arrangements for the work that I want you to do. It will be work that you like to do."

Dad struggled to understand what had just happened. As the newest arrival at Mount Rushmore and having no friends or confidants to discuss this upsetting news with, Dad poured out his disbelief and fears to Mother the only way possible: by pen and paper.

The last line of Dad's April first letter to Mother summed it up: "We should see [it's a] national holiday—april fools day."

Mother's reply to this unexpected news was penned on April 6, 1936, and reveals her penchant for getting to the point:

Why aren't you working in your own line of work? Talk to Borglum and let him know your efficiencies. Think clearly, dear, be diplomatic but please go to the point and be systematic about it. You must know definitely what you are there for, how long and all about it. Go to Borglum's place yourself. Be business-like. It is your right to know where and how you stand and to have some sort of a guarantee. You have a family and for that reason you must know . . . is your job to continue to be mathematical?

Mother encouraged my father to face the reality of the situation and to find a book that would teach him all about surveying.

Dad, meanwhile, was attempting to face his fear of heights

and ascend the mountain to take measurements. He reported on April 5 that he had to go up to 6,200 feet on that granite mountain and familiarize himself with the four heads of the presidents. He wrote: "I was on all the levels, imagine me up there, but I did it. What a sight. I hope I can take you up some time."

A few days later, he reported that he had been up on the mountain all morning, drawing. "They tried to have me go out on a harness," he confided, "but I would not. Let them laugh if they want to, I should worry, you know how I like going on high spots." Dad had already written Mother about the "poor men that work up on the mountain. I cannot see how they stand it, the dust, the noise, and the dizzy altitude. The way they hang on the side of the mountain in harnesses is enough to scare a man to death. Well I suppose they too must eat."

Perhaps Dad's letter of April 3 provided the most detail about how hard life had become for him:

Just received your letter dated Mar 30. I will try and answer all of your questions to the best of my ability. I think some of them I have answered in one of my early letters. . . . I feel lost and forsaken. Sometime the best of us feel tired and we wonder why life has so many sides. The two nights on the train were weary. And as for giving Borglum your respects, I [am] sorry but [I] can not at present—I have not seen him. Mama, chances of coming here are very [scarce]. It all depends on what Borglum has up his sleeves. There are twenty to forty I guess. Most of them live at Keystone, with their families. There are two families living here—the caretaker and his wife with a small daughter about two years old—and the fellow that runs the eating place and about three or four single fellows that board there. There are no accommodations. My dorm is the office, they are still working on it. It is a new building and I hope I can stay here. And I used to think that little window you used to open was much, you ought to see here, well, ice forms in your ears. The meals, well lets not talk about them. I do hope Borglum [will] make it worth while [but] I am afraid not. The wages here seem to me very small. I am going to ask about my expenses when I see Borglum. Wouldn't you?

Well let us hope he comes tomorrow.

To day has been a very cold day wind blowing and icy—no work on the mountain today. I as usual at the studio. Gee I hope I [have a] good math book. I wonder if we could get that book the Wise & Co published—fun with figures—and short cuts in mathematics. It surely would help out here. What am I to do, if the salary is small? Think of it seven dollars go every week for eats—whether I eat or not. . . .

This my dear is a weary life, I hope I may be able to sculpture with Borglum, that may help. There is no play all work and more work—up at 6:30—to work at 7:30 work until 12:00 one half hour for lunch and back to work, until 4:00 wash eat and that is all. No where to go—if you go to Keystone which is 3 miles away it will cost you money—drink and what not. So the best is to go to your room and listen to the clicking clock—I never did like clocks but now I do—it's the only thing that breaks the emptiness of this lonesome place. It's a good thing I have you to write to, it is like talking to you with my very soul.

I walked up the road, we did, to day and thought how wonderful yesterday was and how cruel to day can be. Of course the scene was different, it was as cold, can be the wind was so strong it allmost threw us off the side of the mountain. It's very cold in my room, the wind outside is blowing to beat the band. What is great about this place is the outside John—boy if I get use to this nothing will hurt me. No way one can take a bath

In completing his work as a surveyor, Dad climbed higher than he could have imagined.

Dad checks the topography of the area by hiking around the mountain.

only with a small can of water. Well it's a good thing I have the prayer for today. "O God give me courage to live another day. Let me not turn coward before its difficulties or prove recreant to its duties. Let me be sweet and sound at heart, in spite of ingratitude, treachery, or meanness. Preserve me, O God, from minding little stings, or giving them. Help me to keep my heart clean, and live so honestly and fearlessly that no outward failure can dishearten me, or take away the joy of conscious integrity. Open wide the eyes of my soul that I may see good in all things. Grant this day some new vision of thy truths. Inspire me with the spirit of joy and gladness and make me the cup of strength to suffering souls. In the name of [the] strong Deliverer. Amen."

As one who has spent a lifetime in theater and film, I feel qualified in saying that Dad's letters did not give Mount Rushmore good reviews. In fact, the picture he painted was bleak, and his letters were a barometer of his state of mind. The truth was simple, however—he had no other options, no other alternatives.

"I have about $25.00 left," Dad reported to Mother. "I have to pay my board. I pay $7.00 a week for food. As for lodging. I do not know what that is because I sleep at the office." He went on to ask Mother if she needed money and told her not to worry about getting money to him, because, as he said, "It's my job to try and get some to you." Dad informed her that they were paid every two weeks and that it would take an extra week for it to reach them at Mount Rushmore.

At this point in time, little did Dad know that he was not the only one who had money problems.

5 | Making Headway with Borglum

Gutzon Borglum himself was having a financial struggle that was far more serious than Mom and Dad's and, in fact, jeopardized their chances of getting what they needed from the sculptor. Mount Rushmore's fiscal year ended in June, and if Borglum was unable to raise more capital from the government or from other sources, work would come to a complete halt soon thereafter.

In my experience, most artists are not outstanding businessmen. I would not expect an artist to be found at the head of the class in any financial institution. Borglum was a painter and a sculptor, a real artist and an idealist. As one studies the Mount Rushmore project from 1927 to 1941, it becomes apparent that work time on the mountain was full of downtime. Weather conditions were one cause for work being halted, but the absence of the master sculptor, who was scurrying after funds, was another major factor.

From the outset, there were flaws in Gutzon Borglum's plan for paying for the work. In his book *The Carving of Mount Rushmore* (1985), Rex Alan Smith spells out the point quite well in a chapter entitled "Government Aid—Half a Loaf, But Bet-

ter Than None." Smith reported on a meeting between the sculptor and the United States president at the dedication of the site in 1927 when, Borglum said: "President [Calvin] Coolidge whispered to me, 'Who's paying for all this?'" Borglum responded, "'These farmers are paying for it.'" To which, the president replied: "'These people cannot do this and they ought not to be asked to do it. . . . You come see me when I get back to Washington . . . and we will set down and work out a plan'" (p. 172).

Borglum, however, wanted to finance the work with non-federal funds. After all, he had many well-to-do supporters, was used to raising money, and liked meeting the public. It fit his style. It also meant that control of the money remained in his hands. But was he a good businessman? Not everyone thought so. A prominent magazine owner named Herbert Myrick, who "was awed by Borglum's sculptural ability," nevertheless conceded that Borglum was prone "to 'blow in' in one way or another" any funds he got his hands on, a failing, Myrick added, that was common to all "creative geniuses" (Smith, p. 126). In spite of Borglum's preference for private funding, the South Dakota congressional delegation, with President Coolidge's support, introduced a bill for $250,000 in federal matching funds, and in 1929, the project finally took off.

Borglum was thus often away from the mountain trying to raise money either from friends or from the politicians in Washington, D.C., causing work to stop until he secured new funding. Historians suggest that the sculptor began work in 1927 with less than ten percent of his proposed budget in hand. Finally, in 1934, President Franklin D. Roosevelt placed Mount Rushmore under the National Park Service, and Congress appropriated funds that required no match, but Borglum continued to be an idealist rather than a businessman, and government funding came in fits and starts as other national needs became more pressing. In the end,

over eighty-five percent of the nearly one million dollars spent on Mount Rushmore would come from the federal government.

In addition to Borglum's absences, weather conditions also influenced progress on the mountain. Dad reported "winds so strong that they nearly threw the men off the side of the mountain." On April 10, he wrote: "When I came out it was snowing to beat the band and it is not as cold as it has been but no one can tell, the weather changes so." He later lamented: "Here we are April 16, 1940, and about 12" of snow. All is covered with snow. The power lines are down and we are out of lights." This pattern of unsettled and extreme weather would repeat itself throughout the month of April. Dad made it clear to Mother that if the workers did not ascend the mountain, they did not get paid—a heavy

making headway with borglum | 59

(*left*)
Frank Skells ventures outdoors to check the snow depth.

(*right*)
One of the buildings, possibly the office, can be seen through the snowflakes of a Mount Rushmore snowstorm.

Dad attempts a smile while looking out over the deep Black Hills snow.

burden when money was always at the forefront of everyone's concerns.

Offsetting the gloomy mood brought on by the adverse weather conditions were days when the beauty of nature and gorgeous weather inspired Dad: "You should see this sight—one cannot image these immense spruce trees laden with heavy snow, the smaller one bends to the ground, a masterpiece of beauty only God could conceive. A deep silence, the tree at attention all dressed in white guarding the mystery of the hill they stand on. The sun has appeared giving them life, but near are the big clouds to spoil the party."

Juxtaposed against these poetic thoughts, however, was the raw reality of their financial situation, coupled with the frustration over the terrible physical conditions and the prospect of doing work he had not been hired to do. At this point, Dad's letters were sounding more and more discouraged, as if he was entertaining the possibility of leaving the mountain and returning home. By mid-April, a number of his letters focused on making contact with people in Rochester who might help him get a job if the Mount Rushmore project did not work out.

He spoke of writing to two school administrators who had hired him earlier to teach art classes in Rochester and about getting information from the Borglums:

I have made up my mind. I must write to Mrs. Moore and to Mr. Bird. . . . What are we to do? God what a mess I have placed you and the children [in].

Darling do be careful. Don't work too hard. Ok! Mama I am sick and very tired of it all. I must have a long talk with Borglum, if I have to tie him up. I cannot see how you can come here on what I'll be making. Conditions are not favorable here. Darling I would rather die than subject you to all this; it would

We did our best to help Mother shovel snow back home in Avon.

kill you and the children, no that would never do. So please consider all. There must be an answer to all this I will find it. Well with these two letters I have received today—makes the total letter received to date 15.

Well I see little Arty is writing to his daddy now. Not bad—It is wonderful—Gee he [is] some boy—Why not find a small house in Avon for you and the children. I'll send money to you as soon as I receive it, no check yet I'll have about 95 hours no its 104 hours they pay until today 13 days. What would you advise to do darling? Gee I miss you sweetheart and need you, but we must be brave and fight. Not so bad I sound like you mama. Oh! mama I cannot write my side aches so, its my left side. It's the weather I think. All day we have had rain and snow and its quite cold. The whole world seems upside down. Work—work for what end—maybe things will change but how can they. LB [Lincoln Borglum] is just a big kid—what a racket they are pulling—artist and sculptor free. I would not dare write all, but I am answering much and will tell you someday.

I will talk to GB [Gutzon Borglum] tell him all and tell him what he promised me. He must listen. Well there goes another spot of ink, don't blame me it's the pen. Well I owe about 17.00 to date, figure up how much it nets me being here. You must forgive this letter my mind will not give, its in a whirl my eyes ache and my heart. Give my love to the children and you, words fail to express my deep love and affection I have for you. Well, I did write the letter, but I see they are no good now. I'll write to Todd and send it to you, you see it and send it back. Goodnight my love.

A full two weeks into Dad's stay, the words *wait* and *waiting* appeared frequently in the love letters. He was *waiting* for Borglum to show up. And just as in the play *Waiting for Godot* by

Samuel Beckett, Dad thought that when Borglum showed up, all the problems would be resolved. Mother's queries were always based on the hope that we children and she could join Dad in South Dakota. "Have you talked with Gutzon Borglum about the future," she asked Dad, "for we need to be together as a family."

Unfortunately, Dad's replies were not what Mother wanted to hear: "Saw GB today. I was at work, at the studio. A warm greeting and out he went—no chance to talk to him. . . . I must know where I stand." Another time he wrote: "It's the same old story. I have not had the chance to talk to GB he was in for a minute today and out he went." Or, "I have tried to talk to him but he is always with a group."

Dad's frustration continued to grow until one day he decided that he was going to make an appointment with Borglum right away, even if he had to "walk to his ranch at Hermosa, about 25 miles away." He followed this comment later with, "if I have to tie him down to get him to listen," an idea he had already expressed in an earlier April letter. Finally, Dad's response to his dilemma was to change tactics, to be cool and disguise his feelings. So, in spite of his own personal fears and concerns about the dangers posed by climbing up and over the mountain, he forged ahead.

His letter of April 10 revealed his changing attitude:

There is much to be gained if I use my head, also much to learn, something that may change the course of my life. He is a great person, and the name and association will mean a lot to me. I will have to do a lot of studying and planning if I wish to succeed. . . . you must realize the whole set up is new to me.

The work, the people, I must get used to things. The experience alone out here is worth a million dollars to me. You can never know maybe I too will carve mountains some day. . . . I must learn, yes learn all the tricks he knows and maybe more.

In attempting to adjust to not getting what he had expected from Gutzon Borglum, Dad continued: "He is old, I need to learn, and I am young—I cannot be head strong. I must be calm. . . . I have so much work to do. I don't know where to begin. Well, one must be patient and suffer."

Even though Dad's letters to Mother were likely to vent his frustrations concerning his Mount Rushmore experience, a letter to someone else would take on a different tone. Dad wrote to Mother's sister and brother-in-law, painting a rosier picture:

Dear Georgia and Jack,
Well, I am in the beautiful hills of South Dakota, yes a real

Gutzon Borglum focuses on his masterpieces as he ascends the mountain in the bucket and the Black Hills fold out behind him. Image by Bell Photo. South Dakota State Historical Society

Hilly Billy. Thanks a million for your sweet letter. It brought love to my tired eyes. It surely was wonderful to hear from you. Remember, one becomes quite lonesome away from the ones he or she loves, not bad hey! I am working at the studio reproducing a map of all the park area—including the figures on the mt. and all the buildings—stairs and all—a real headache. It takes a lot of thought and I have to do a lot of surveying. This work moves the soul to be bound in these beautiful Black Hills. Its just ducky, you and Jack must come up sometime and visit this amazing region.

From the top of the heads you can view all of the Black Hills. One is about 6,300 feet above sea level, a sight the gods behold. The work they are doing here is indeed phenomenal, it is an immortal work of art and engineering. Ha, I am helping people make history. Here in the beautiful Black Hills, history is being born and preserved ideals of America. For this region tinged with the romance of pioneer day infused with the spirit of adventure reflects the America of heroic yesterday. These gigantic figures of Washington, Jefferson, Lincoln and Theodore Roosevelt carved with granite will for eternity of time gaze down upon the America of tomorrow and leave a record of today—I hope you may visit this amazing region someday. The heads are facing southeast—you travel from the hoist house below to the top of the mountains. On the top there is what they call a wench house. The ride up moves the soul. I was up Saturday again making my second time up the mountain—walked up and down all the heads. It surely takes the breath away. I did not ride down, I walked so that I could survey the surrounding country side. There are 600 stairs down. The proposed new steps are in drawing form. The poor fellows that drill on the mt. I cannot see how they stand it, the dust and height, it's enough to scare a man to death.

Meanwhile, Mother's letters began to express her growing maternity needs and her conviction that the new baby would be a girl. At the same time, she continued to deal with the uncertainties of Dad's situation:

APRIL 9–APRIL 11

We are to have a little girl. If I am to come out there to be with you, traveling after the 4th or 5th month will be difficult, especially with two active children. Very difficult under any circumstance. Now don't treat this lightly please, it is very serious. Being with you when I have the baby is the only thing I think about . . . find out about maternity Doctors in Rapid City.

APRIL 12

Yes, we are to have a baby. He's told you you would have a future there. . . . you see you must talk to Borglum and have an understanding. Tell him I am expecting a baby so you must do some planning. You must have a guarantee of work for at least a year. A family can't move 2,000 miles without prospects, especially with the woman pregnant. . . . He told you you would have a future there.

Even as Mother struggled to get a complete picture of Dad's life in South Dakota, she also mixed in good advice, wisdom, and love:

APRIL 13

Every place you go darling you will find many snakes in the grass and crude people. Just keep your eyes opened, avoid political discussions. Be a good listener, especially avoid talking factory and about those you work for. It is bad policy.

Fri. April 18, 1940
Avon, N.Y.

Dear Art,

I was pleased & disappointed with your letter this morning. Pleased because you are getting #.65 an hour. That is not bad Art really. Remember you are just beginning. That work is new to you. Really I'm pleased about it. However I'm very disappointed because of the attitude you have taken toward your employer. I warned you against that. That is the very thing Fran said would happen - inferring that you would never get any place with any body because that is the way you are. Art dear, I was hoping you would prove otherwise. Please try to take the advice I wrote in yesterday's letter. It is so easy to find fault for every human person is full of faults - you, I the next person. Think how easy is to think each member of your fame is a rat, Fran, any of us yet you have to tolerate. There too, Art, in fact any where you will have to tolerate plenty. The sooner you learn to be wise about it, make the most of it and avoid any sour feeling, the sooner you will forge ahead. Mark my word Art. You will never get anywhere as long as you have the feelings you have about your employer. If you are ever an employer yourself you will understand a few things. Please try to be patient & understanding Art & hold that infernal tongue of yours. You can become angry, blow off at your family - but not others so watch your step. Go ahead for things, get your proper rewards when you have proved you deserve them, but do it diplomatically & in a friendly manner - or you lose. Be friendly & understanding with G.B. Art. He has an awful burden on his shoulders Art & there are plenty trying to make it hard for him & plenty who are ungrateful. Please don't cypher out each fault & dwell on it. See the fine things he has done & is doing & praise them. Please art develope that attitude. It will mean more toward your wellfare than all the talents you have put to-gither. Can't you see that dear?! Attitude attitude, the feeling for G.B. & not against him. That is what is going to mean so much to you. Really Art it broke my heart to read - "sculptor, director - fine." That has always been your attitude

toward someone & it is
your downfall. Please try
hard to change it Art.
Inside of you, your feelings
on all these things must
change before you even
have a chance to succeed. Fight
on the positive side so you can
grow. A negative fight is a
losing one. You can't be a good
man as you think you are,
until that is accomplished.
Art I hate to have to preach so
much but I realize deep down so
many more things than you do.

My mother was a wonderful
teacher. I have been taught these
things from the cradle. Thirty
years of experience has proved them.
You see I have been conscious of such
things having had them brought
to my attention while you haven't.
Art just such attitudes has made
the man who seems not very
smart, not talented, in fact, the
very ordinary person succeed
while sometimes men with
brilliant minds, many talents
fail failed fall because they lacked
the understanding of just a few

of these little things that are
so important. Art, please let
me help you where I can for I
love you dearly. I don't want to
see you on a Lewis St. scale & that
will be where you will always
belong if you don't change. These
are bitter words to you Art, but
they are a lot more bitter to me,
for I have had faith in you —
even when others have said
you would never succeed
because your mind is wrong —
meaning your attitudes towards
people & things.

Art, I sincerely believe you
have done the right thing by
going out there & I sincerely
believe there is a future there
for you. Stick & be patient. Your
salary is O.K. for a start dear so
don't be unhappy. The next important
thing is what are your chances for
remaining there any length of time.
If you are sure you are to be there
we will move to Rapid City. It
won't be any more expensive living
there then there so why shouldn't
we be to-gether at least on Sundays?
And Art dear, I have good news.

Good night darling. I miss you very much and want to be with you even with an outside toilet.

In some cases, my parents' letters crossed in the mail. Dad's April fourteenth letter revealed the bluntness of his encounter with his boss, Gutzon Borglum: "He promised and he didn't. He claims he must see first what I can do. . . . [He says] one must earn his way . . . and as for family, there is no place for them." Here, Borglum was referring to existing conditions at Mount Rushmore as being inhospitable.

In his April seventeenth letter, my father concurred with Borglum's assessment:

Darling, you insist on coming here. That my dear is almost impossible at present. There is no place we could get. The thing [is that] we will know in about two weeks whether we work this summer or not. It is not so easy to make $50 a week. Maybe someday. But right now I am rated at 65 cents per hour. I talked to Lincoln today. He was much surprised at what his father had promised. He surely seems to be a good sport and is going to see if he can have it changed a bit. He does not advise the family moving here at present. I will know more about [things] to-morrow. You understand, darling, I would do anything to have you with me. We should all be together but things cannot be. We must think of our children, and this life would not be fit for you darling. I pray I will be in a position to change this in the near future.

This environment would not be a new start. It would be the end. I will see about the guarantee, but that is in the hands of God.

We must not hurry. We must think and think hard. Yes, GB did tell me he needed more money, without it the whole work will fold up.

I can only imagine how that last sentence must have made my mother feel.

Mount Rushmore,
April 30. 1940

Dear Mary,

You know darling I want you to help me, and "to" correct my mistakes. after all you are my wife and pal and helper. I need you very much, and thank you for your help. I need your advice, it really Mary mean a lot to me

Darling I made a statement to this effect. I have painted some of the unfinished things like a little shelf I had build and some of the hangers. When we have a good day I will take a photo of my room and also one of the studio. I have done nothing about a bed as yet. I will find one some where or make one. I have asked a lad if he had one and he said he will look, but still there will be the bed clothes, but time will tell. Where there is a will there is a way. I am going to stay here - its the only place that makes live worth living. I talk with L. B. and all is O.K. of course Frank does not mind. So that will take care of my room.

I saw the proposed - project with the hall of records and what not - it surely is a big job and a long one - if it is ever acted upon.

Darling the work that I am doing at the studio - is this - I carve in plaster. I am doing miniature of all the park areas.

6 | A Sensitive Subject

My father, Arthur J. Cerasani, was extremely sensitive to the fact that he had never received a college education. Even as a youth he had often missed high-school classes so he could work and provide money for his parents and siblings. That was unfortunate and also illegal, but it was necessary. As the Italian saying goes, "It is all about the family." Dad was the oldest, and he tried to follow that dictum, even at the cost of hurting his educational prospects.

Dad did not have much say in the matter because my grandfather Luigi had a different view on education. Luigi was a good accountant with bad health and language limitations and thus had difficulty finding employment. As the head of the household, Luigi held strictly to the principle that everyone worked to help the family. The family story is that even when a court judge, seeing great merit in Dad's abilities, offered him a Harvard education, my grandfather's answer was a firm "No."

Dad was self-taught in much of what he did, and he was an avid reader. He claimed Leonardo da Vinci and Michelangelo as his heroes, so he was pleased when Lincoln Borglum brought him

In addition to creating a model of the park, Dad worked on small plaster heads to be sold to tourists.

He also made profile casts of President Franklin D. Roosevelt.

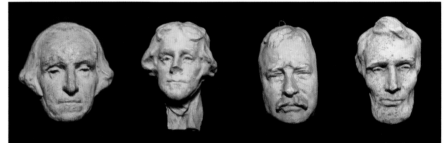

a set of books concerning those artists' writings and work. Dad's greatest weakness was his writing. The hundreds of letters he wrote home to my mother fully revealed his language deficiencies, especially in grammar and spelling.

Mother, ever the schoolteacher, was always correcting him out of a desire to advance his station in life. For example, she wrote to him about his correspondence with someone else: "Send it to me first for check up for you make terrible mistakes, dear. She would consider you illiterate if you send her a letter such as most of yours are, so do be careful."

In defense of Dad, one could make the case that he was trying to express himself and often had to write in less than ideal conditions. As he described them, those conditions included being "often in a room with no heat . . . no writing table"; "writing under bed covers in a bed to handle the cold"; "little light"; "tired eyes from working on miniature models"; and "leaking pens." Then, too, he reminded Mother, "the altitude is 5,700 where I am staying, it hurts the ears."

Two other letters described the pesky bugs that also made writing a challenge:

MAY 31
I have been trying for about two hours to write this letter, my room my desk seems to be filled with small green and black flying bugs they are driving me crazy. I cannot even move my pen there are so many. God only knows how they got here. Of course today must have brought them, it's really been very hot and was that sun hot, a real summer's day.

JUNE 1
All is well darling, but these small pests most of them I destroyed—but there are many still flying around, but I will fix their water wagon.

The poor physical conditions my father described, along with inadequate formal education, became a recipe for hurt feelings. Mother's desire to improve his writing was well intentioned, but it wounded Dad's ego. His response to her criticism was not in the least surprising—a combination of "poor me" and realistic bluntness:

Mount Rushmore
Dear Mary,
Maybe it would be better, if I stop writing to you. It is very difficult to read letters written by an illiterate person. Mary it is very hard for a person to write when he has so very much on his mind. I never go over my letter once they have been written. So! Most of your letters have been—please do this, you make a mistake, oh! how illiterate you are—and please spell Mary with an M—and this and that, please forgive this but sometimes ones nerves just go. I thank you for great interest in my welfare and I am sorry for my mistakes. Please remember, I am doing things that are new to me. It takes all my time planning and thinking, that is the reason I have not written to any one but you, a few letters home—Much love to you and the children.
Always,
Arthur

Another letter offered a more conciliatory tone, "You know darling I want you to help me, and to correct my mistakes—after all you are my wife and pal and helper."

A response from Mother illustrates her typically practical style:

Darling, if I talk about your letters, it is for your own good. I would love you just as much if you made one million mistakes, but others don't forgive and they are very harsh in

their judgment. You have a wonderful opportunity right now
to learn to write correctly and spell correctly. There will come a
time when you will have to write an important letter and won't
have time to send it to me for a checkup. Then, when you are
[censured], you will wish you had taken my advice.

Sometimes I really can't make out your meaning. A little extra
time & pains would correct that & it would be well worth the
time and effort. I don't criticize to be mean but to help you avoid
trouble in the future, dear. Your letters are a wonderful help to
me. I look forward to them each day & am very disappointed if I
don't receive one.

Ironically, Mother wanted more letters and more details, but she needed to be reminded that they would include more errors. In her May sixteenth letter, she asked Dad several questions about his work and ended with the comment: "You really explain so little, Art. More, please." In what can be considered a conciliatory gesture, Dad wrote: "When I return home, I'll take 6 easy lessons from you so that I may write better letters." Acceptance of each other seemed to have been reached, and that would serve them well during the difficult period of separation.

7 | A Loving Wife with Good Advice

hroughout the ups and downs of their days apart, my parents, Arthur and Mary Cerasani, revealed a hardiness of soul and a wisdom almost beyond their years. My mother especially waxed practical as the following letter indicates. Of course, my father had a philosophical side that he sometimes showed as well.

> *Avon, New York/Monday, April 8, 1940*
> *Dear Art,*
> *Darling, please don't be discouraged. It is just unfortunate that you weren't brought up to be independent and self-reliant. The experience you are having is so much harder for you because of that, which means you must fight all the harder to overcome that deficiency in yourself. Besides, dear, good roads are not all straight.*
> *There are lots of turns and by ways to worthwhile places. Most places think you are greatly honored to be called out there by Borglum. Imagine what they would think should you fail. Don't let us down, darling. I know it is easy to talk, but do fight, Papa. Borglum is busy. Don't wait for him to come to you. Go to him or when you see him*

tell him you would like to talk to him and ask him what time would be convenient for him. By all means don't write to him when so close. Go right to him regardless of the difficulties. Just make that a point. If you sit back waiting for people to come to you, you will never get anywhere. Nor would anyone think anything of you. Be progressive and aggressive, Papa. Go after life. You have lots to do and lots to do with. Life should never be boring for you, even out there, unless you relax and permit it to be.

Be a man of courage, darling. I know you were never taught that, but you do have the materials. Please don't let history repeat itself. It can happen to you. Don't be mistaken about that. How I wish I could be with you, Papa, to help you for I have plenty of self-reliance but not the materials you have. And if I were with you, you wouldn't have the chance to develop the self-reliance you otherwise have. So please, Papa, show yourself a man even though it be hard. Don't fall into the ways of the common man. Spend those spare hours pushing yourself. Get someone to take you to Borglum's ranch. How far away is it? Remember dear, it is only through your own efforts that you are going places, and those efforts must continue even when everything seems to be against you. I hate to preach so much, dear, but I do it because I know how true what I am saying is.

Dickie is sitting on a chair beside me calling "Ma—Ma" in loud tones. Every time I look at him he breaks forth in a grin from ear to ear, eyes glow and his whole face beaming. He is so wonderful and Arty too.

And I fear there will be another one next November. So you must fight, darling, not just do your work but push yourself. Talk to Borglum to find out where you stand now and what your possibilities are. Should he ever shove you aside, don't be daunted, go right back. Be insistent until you know what you

Gutzon Borglum and other men work on the head of Lincoln. South Dakota State Historical Society

want to know. Don't let him think you are classed with the rest of those people there, Papa. You know what he said about them.

Arthur, I will tell you what good you are to yourself out there. . . . You are having the chance to either prove yourself a man, forge ahead by pushing yourself entirely by your own efforts, or of sinking to the level of those people who are content to drink, play pool, and live as they do.

It is your opportunity and it is a difficult one, but it is up to you whether you fall as one behind . . . or whether you forge ahead. I can't understand why you don't go to see Borglum yourself. Never wait for anybody or anything. . . .

Keep going. Don't give yourself a chance or time to think or to wonder what it is all about. Plan your work, your studies, etc. Think of [Admiral Richard E.] Byrd in Little America [Antarctic outpost] all alone. There is a man who has courage, a real man. Papa, you can be one too. . . .

You have an opportunity now, take hold. Don't wait. See Borglum, see him if you have to break into his ranch to do so. I love you too much to see you fall by the way side, to think of you as the rest—jelly, no backbone.

Please, Papa, in your next letter tell me of your plans for the future . . . your salary. Present ideas to Borglum, tell him you want a big enough salary so we can come out there and live in Rapid City. Don't give in without a good fight.

Forgive the preaching, Papa, but you break my heart staying there in the dark a whole week as though you were a bit of machinery put to work rather than an individual who went 2,000 miles for something he isn't getting. Get busy and talk to Borglum. What about the factory?

You have lots to think of, Art. I hope you aren't making a mistake and letting all that take care of itself. It will be against you.

A more confident Arthur Cerasani edges down the mountain. On April 21, 1940, he wrote, "As time goes on I'll surely become a dear old dare devil."

I sent your Architects and Builders book, camera, and Easter egg today.
Love,
Mary

Subsequent letters in April included Mother's wise advice as she attempted to stabilize my father and help him "stick it out" in what he had perceived to be a hostile environment.

Dear Art,

. . . Most great men are very unreasonable in some respects.
Please, dear, don't let this again be your downfall. People are full
of mistakes. Win the man GB in spite of his unreasonableness.
. . . Be patient, be tolerant, be kind, avoid discussions against GB
and people who talk against him. . . . Praise his work, Papa. He
no doubt has a very difficult job and is working against many
odds. Don't always believe the grouch. For once believe in the
man you are working for no matter what happens. Show that
you believe in him. Don't stand off. Be active in this belief. . . .
Dear, in spite of all try to have faith in the man you are working
for. . . . He gave you the job, regardless how small, not those peo-
ple who try to turn your mind against him. . . .

In her Wednesday, April twenty-fourth letter, Mother continued to exhort my father:

Dear Art,
The article you spoke of about Borglum is condensed in the
May Reader's Digest. It is written in a rather sarcastic tone. I
will try to get it soon and send it to you. It is the type of man
Borglum is.¹ However, darling, please remember all I have told
you. Be on the good side of him. An important person is bound to
have much written about him. For every ounce of truth, pounds
of exaggeration and falsehood. Keep your ears and eyes opened
but still be diplomatic and on his side. The article says he plans
to model 25 heads of important Americans and make [friezes]
depicting western civilization from the beginning.² If he likes
you, it will pay you to be by him. At least, dear, don't fail in an
attempt. His plans are colorful and as the article said he couldn't
possibly finish it in his lifetime.
Art, try to study sculpting with that man. Keep your head. You

1. The article, "The Man
Who Carves Mountains,"
by Samuel Lubell and
Walter Everett, *Reader's
Digest* (May 1940): 113–15,
described the seventy-
three-year-old Borglum
as "a paunchy man with
a bald head and a brushy
mustache," who "takes
his immortality pretty
seriously." Borglum, in the
presence of tourists, once
"ran up and down
the mountainside so often
. . . that he collapsed, to the
delight of his workmen,
who respect him as an
artist but consider him
a slave driver. Fits of
temperament leave him
with splitting headaches.
When he becomes enraged
at a workman, he fires his
secretary, who returns to
work the next day and tells
him what she did with her
day off" (p. 113).

2. These projects
were part of the Hall of
Records, for which he had
received congressional
appropriations. *See* Lincoln
Borglum, "The Hall of
Records and the Great
Stairway," National Park
Service, nps.gov, and Paul
Higbee, *Mount Rushmore's
Hall of Records* (Keystone,
S.Dak.: Mount Rushmore
History Assoc., 1999).

GUTZON BORGLUM 1867–1941

John Gutzon de la Mothe Borglum was born March 25, 1867, in Saint Charles, Idaho. He started his career as a painter and studied in Paris for about ten years. In 1901, he returned to America, determined to start afresh as a sculptor.

On the ship back to the United States, he met Mary Montgomery, a young American who had just finished her Ph.D. at the University of Berlin. She became his second wife, and they settled into a house in Connecticut that they called Borgland.

Borglum's talent for sculpting was soon recognized, and in 1915 the United Daughters of the Confederacy commissioned him to carve a monument to the Confederacy on Stone Mountain, in Georgia. The Stone Mountain project dissolved amid financial disputes, and Borglum fled the situation to work on a new project in the Black Hills of South Dakota.

While the Mount Rushmore project was plagued with money problems, many workers realized the historical significance of the work and the opportunity it offered. "Indeed with the spirit of adventures, history is in the making," Arthur Cerasani wrote to his wife on April 27, 1940; "America will be proud of the work that is being done here."

Borglum meant to create a monument for the ages, and he brought the personality of a titan to this goal. Prone to stubbornness and perfectionism, Borglum's temperament led to many confrontations. Sometimes he fired his best men, whom his son Lincoln then re-hired. Borglum's personal energy and vision were unmatched, however. He climbed Mount Rushmore and the surrounding mountains to determine the best way in which to carve the stone faces. He traveled the world to meet politicians and celebrities, looking for support.

Gutzon Borglum died suddenly on March 6, 1941, from complications following surgery.

LINCOLN BORGLUM 1912–1986

Lincoln Borglum was born on April 9, 1912, in Stamford, Connecticut. He was at his father's side when Gutzon Borglum selected the site for the four presidents. Gutzon made certain that his son was trained in all aspects of the Mount Rushmore operations. Lincoln started out in the project's early days as a part-time volunteer. By 1933 he was a full-time pointer, and in 1938 he began to supervise all work on the mountain.

After Gutzon Borglum's death on March 6, 1941, Lincoln Borglum assumed the responsibility to finish what his father had left incomplete. From 1941 to 1943, Lincoln served as the first superintendent of Mount Rushmore National Memorial.

While much has been written about his father being temperamental, hard to get along with, and often unapproachable, just the opposite could be said about Lincoln. Workers often turned to him for advice and information about the work to be performed, and his sociable character made him a favorite. "L. B is going to bring L. Di Vinci's new note book so that I may read it," Arthur Cerasani wrote to his wife. "We get a long fine he seems to be a real person." Before leaving for work one morning, Arthur wrote, "I hope L. B. comes—he has been ill and he also is a great guy."

After leaving Mount Rushmore, Lincoln Borglum moved to Texas, and his sculptures grace several churches there. He died in Corpus Christi on January 27, 1986.

must be in on that. He has already had some consent of a senate committee or some such. I'm not sure just what, for I haven't the article here. Darling, an ambitious man no matter how talented or perfect will have all kinds of jealousies and sneering so don't be daunted. Realizing these things, go ahead, learn all you can and wait your chance to get in on some plans. Watch each step and should a tantrum he display, don't lose your control. A man of his sort is apt to be temperamental, but might repent the next minute or forget, so even in an extreme case don't be so hasty to judge. Again I say be understanding and sympathetic in the light of keeping your head and with the hopes of getting next to him. Never be influenced by gossip.

Love,
Mary

Mother's letters proved to be timely and full of good advice, which served Dad well during his stay at Mount Rushmore. They certainly lent credence to a saying I've heard all my life: "Behind every great man is a great woman." Dad knew he had a lot to learn, and getting advice from someone who loved him made the pill a little easier to swallow. Gutzon Borglum, however, was not an easy man to get "next to."

The first couple of weeks in April 1940 laid bare the difficulties my parents faced and would be facing for an indefinite period of time. Their need to communicate kept them in close touch with each other by mail, but the time it took for a letter to circulate round trip was too long and often resulted in frustration. In 1940, a letter sent could sit in a local post office for days due to inclement weather. Phone and telegram services were not readily available, and if they were, the cost was prohibitive.

The separation from Dad had caused Mother great distress right from the beginning, and she had let her needs be known. Ever practical, Mother implored my father to write more frequently as the antidote to the frustrating delays:

> *Darling, do please write every day. This tension is dreadful. I wait, each day, hoping for good news, or at least an explanation of what is happening. Do explain things more in detail and please remember, it takes 3 days for one to get here and 3 more days for my letter to get back to you and one in answering, which in all makes one week.*

At first, the distance (over two thousand miles) that separated my parents from each other did not register with me as that great of an obstacle. However, as I read passages from early letters, I was able to put their situation into proper perspective and became more sensitive to the level of discomfort, pain, anxiety, and stress they were experiencing. Certainly in today's milieu, with cell phones offering email, texting, and instant messaging, one can become jaded and take communication for granted. However, once I stepped out of my own time capsule and into theirs, the struggles began to resonate with me.

I was especially moved by my father's expressive words in numerous letters:

Mount Rushmore
Dear Mary,

. . . I need the warmth of your heart, the feel of your lips. I need the life only you can give me, the fulfillment of my dream, the inspiration of my soul. . . . My heart is not so good. I am lonesome, sad, and unhappy out here all alone. With spring in the air, the beginning of life with no Mary. Without you, life is not life. . . .

. . . I miss not seeing you and not having you close to me. I awake with a piece of me missing. To hear your voice and hold you close to my heart, what wouldn't I give. . . .

. . . Oh mama how I love you and miss you. If only I had a magic carpet I would be there in a jiff. . . .

Letters from Mother were equally expressive and full of passion:

Avon
Dearest Art,

Believe me, darling, I wish I were right there to give you my love in person. . . . Gee darling I miss you so and love you so, how I need you and want you to be with me. . . . I love you and hope we can be together soon.

. . . Darling, I miss you much more than anyone could ever miss anyone, and as for loving you, I love you so much I'm a nervous wreck. How is that? My thoughts, my energy, my all. . . . I don't even have enough energy to be sensible. Of course I have no one to fight with and to argue with and everything is quite peaceful, but in spite of that, I would a thousand times prefer to be with you. . . .

. . . Darling, I miss you so and love you so. I do pray that this experience will build you and do you a world of good.

Mount Rushmore's setting aided Dad in filling his letters with imagery to describe his loneliness during the first weeks away from home. South Dakota State Historical Society

Several letters from Dad began to take on a dream-like quality:

Dear Mary,

. . . I hope you were walking with me last night. The big stones that guard the secret of years, all along the side of the road casting a shadow the pine trees stretching towards the heavens, trying to greet the moon, stars everywhere—some small some large and a few trying to send as much light as the moon the air very quiet and parts of the sky a deep blue with a cloud here and there.

Indeed a beautiful sight only God could conceive. How lonesome one becomes walking with such a beautiful set, and no darling, no mama with me so one could hold hands and when the moon was out looking about a kiss on the lips of your darling. . . .

Another time, he wrote:

Good morning my darling—of course some where in the world there must be a good morning. Believe it or not April, and what a sight the wind is blowing hard the trees sway back and forth while from the sky comes fine snow flakes, so thick are they one can not see far, and in one hour all is being covered again.

It must be wonderful to live where spring is trying to grow flowers—rather than snow flakes. Our little snow flakes are having a good time first the wind blows them one way then the other just like life blows some people, but sooner or later they have their way. Either rest on the trees or fall on the stones below. . . . I was up them golden steps again yesterday. I most of the time go up on the mountain by the open bucket but no one works on Sunday—so up I went—up the steps, what a climb it is, puff—puff—up and up—hoping to reach the top, when you are on the top your legs seem empty and shaky. The air is fine and the wind seems to blow harder but it is worth it—for one is very close to heaven and the scenes are very good for the soul it is getting time to depart. Is my lunch ready darling? Thanks a lot—Oh! I must hurry or I'll be late. Oh! What did you say?

I almost forgot to kiss you? I should say not. I keep that for the last because then I start with a print of your lip on my lips and nothing can stop me from fighting hard. So I must go now but I'll be back soon. Goodbye darling—keep well and strong. . . .

The hardship that distance imposed on my parents could not be illustrated any more poignantly than by the text of their letters in the week between April twenty-first and twenty-eighth. Prior to these letters, Mother often mentioned symptoms related to early pregnancy such as nausea, headaches, backaches, and exhaustion. On April 14, she wrote: "I have been feeling rather woozie lately but guess I had better prepare to be more woozie until Nov. 20th. Oh me, such a life. I need strength." On another day, she wrote: "Many pains in stomach, head and back. I am nervous and tired. Don't worry though, I will feel better in another month. . . . I stayed in bed until after 8 this A.M. I just couldn't get up."

Dad, meanwhile, was sharing the nature of his work with Mother:

Darling the work that I am doing at the studio is this. I carve in plaster. I am cloning a miniature of all the park area. Yes! Mount Rushmore, it is a map about 7½ feet by 5½ feet—made in scale 20 feet to the inch. I have completed the heads now the

"I carve in plaster," Dad wrote to Mother on April 30, 1940. The toothpick staircase he described meanders down the front of the model.

stairs, there are 690 steps. The steps are 4" wide and about 64"
per step and the railing I made are like this ⚓ .

You really should see them so small and what a job. I used
tooth picks cut and held together with some of the cement I use
to mend my glasses. G. B. said they were great—but we must
change them, we are to put the new stairs on this model. It took
me 4 days to work them out.

As he worked, Dad was also looking forward to the wonderful event that was to occur in November. A number of times, he mentioned looking forward to a little girl. He took pleasure in receiving a cigar from coworker Matt Reilly right after his wife had given birth, and he talked about the impending birth of coworker Ray Berg's baby in May. With the arrival of Mother's letter of April 21, all his anticipation came to an end:

Friday my nerves have been pretty raw. My head thumps and
my back and bottom ache terribly and I'm getting pretty weak.
I lost the little thing today.
My stomach has ached all day too. Lib says I may bleed from
two weeks to a month. They all tell me I should be in bed, but I
don't know of anyone adequate enough to take full charge of the
children.

APRIL 22
Little Dickie's temperature was 104-1/2 nearly 105. He threw up
over everything too. . . . I'm really exhausted, dear, so excuse me I
won't write more now. It is 9 p.m. and I have many pains in my
stomach, head and back. I am nervous and tired. Dickie being
sick is keeping me on the go.

Dad stands with coworker Ray Berg (left), who was a driller on the mountain. He and his wife lived in a small two-room cabin with no water or bathroom. "They are expecting a baby in May," Dad told Mother.

APRIL 23

I stayed in bed until eight this a.m. I'm quite tired. My stomach and side have ached all day and of course my back and head, but guess that is to be expected.

By the end of the week, she wrote: "I don't believe in being unhappy, but I would be happier with you. Of course, I miss you very much. Here I am in the huge home all alone, with two tiny boys. I not only miss you, but I need you."

Back on the mountain, my father was trying to process this distressing and unexpected turn of events. Not being there to comfort my mother must have caused him much pain and guilt. He returned a flow of words in short and somewhat awkward phrases: "So no baby . . . I had resigned myself to a dear little girl." His next letter: "What happened? Tell me did you lose the baby or why the curse." And the next: "I am sorry you are having such a hard time. I hoped I could be there to help."

Mother's last reference to the miscarriage is in her May third letter. In response to Dad's question concerning the length of her pregnancy, Mom replied: "Two months. Now that is over, but I am tired."

T. S. Eliot once wrote, "April is the cruelest month." How true that was for my parents. April was a roller-coaster ride as they attempted to deal with all the stresses and hardships, both physical and emotional, of each new day.

Mother sent Dad this photograph of Artie, Mother, and me (Dickie) in April 1940.

hile the month of April was emotionally draining, June third and fourth represented the low point of Dad's stay at Mount Rushmore. Sometimes, just when one thinks that things could not possibly get much worse, they do:

Mount Rushmore
June 3, 1940
Dear Mary,
Well, thank your lucky stars, it was not me, but this morning we had our first big accident, the bucket broke loose with five men [in it]— and down she came. Lucky thing Matt [Reilly, foreman] put a bar of steel through the big wheel [in the hoist house] that brings the bucket up—or they would have all been killed. Two were really hurt, one very serious. It happened about 7:15 this morning. I dreamed that I came down and was hurt last night, so I refused to go up this morning—and this is what did happen. The car the five men were riding on got almost to the top and it [slipped] and down she came a mile a min. The men tried hard to stop it with a hand brake, but no use. The hand brake broke and down they

came, and what blood curdling yells; it hit the flat and one man was thrown right out, and was he a mess. I was up at the studio when it happened.

Talk about Providence! Dad must have realized how fortunate he had been because of his dream the night before. Norman E. ("Hap") Anderson was the worker who sustained the worst injury in this accident. He eventually recovered, and no one died in the fourteen years of construction on Mount Rushmore. To have no fatalities when working at heights up to six thousand feet to reshape a mountain and in the process remove one-half million tons of granite over a fourteen-year span is an incredible achievement.

As I was reading Dad's letter of June third, a light bulb of recollection went on inside my own head. Suddenly, two incidents came to my mind that must have influenced Dad's reluctance to take the bucket up the mountain that fateful day.

First, he had to have remembered a story from when he was a little boy. His sister Clotilda at age seven went to her father and asked him to buy a beautiful dress that she had seen earlier that day at McCurdy's, a downtown store. She had said, "Please buy that dress for my funeral." Her words stunned the family and left them wondering why or how such a request had come about. Nevertheless, upon her pleading, they returned to the store and bought the beautiful dress. A week later, Clotilda died. Her family went into deep shock over her death, which was due to spinal meningitis.

Then, a few years later when my father was in high school, my grandmother had begged my grandfather to keep him home because of a dream she had had. She was certain that her dream meant that something bad was going to happen to her son if he went to school that day. My grandfather dismissed her dream

The bucket or cable car carried men up the mountain.
South Dakota State Historical Society

(*top left*)
The bucket with two passengers approaches the landing platform on top of Roosevelt's head. South Dakota State Historical Society

A derrick on top and a hoist below kept the bucket going up and down. South Dakota State Historical Society

and told my father to go to school. Later that day, there was an accident in the machine shop, and my father lost his second and third fingers. Most likely the family stories of those two premonitions were enough to keep Dad from going up the mountain that June morning.

Dad's letter of June third also mentioned another of his fears related to working at Mount Rushmore. It had to do with a rumor that Gutzon Borglum was thinking about assigning him a job as "assistant pointer." Dad shared his concerns in another letter to Mother on the same day:

Darling, things are getting impossible here. No money and what not, no future, and I don't like it here. I have written to Mr. Jones and Mr. Bird and Mrs. Moore. It's no place for us— so please don't come here. Before long, I will return to you and fight hard for a new start. What I am doing does not please me and I can not earn enough for my family. I have made up my mind to study hard and work for a musical training—there is more money in that and it's better for one. I am afraid they will have me help point on the mountain, and it's dusty and I would really be ruined. One must take so many chances, and I love my family too much to do it for whom?—a man that cannot keep his promises. What would you do, Mary? After all, I am young and I will not waste my health on such a thing, would you? Of course, if you think I should do it, I will. But most of these poor men that are here will not live long—they are a sorry lot. I would rather earn less and be healthy and with my family. I would like to come home as soon as I can manage or have you a better idea—write and tell me. I am very tired and sad tonight darling—and must go to sleep, so goodnight darling, see you in dream land.

An invention of Gutzon Borglum's allowed workers to transfer measurements from scale models onto the mountain. Image by Bell Photo. South Dakota State Historical Society

Always loving you,
Arthur J. Cerasani
A pointer is a man that checkes and marks points so that the driller can drill. Of course, it may not be, but if it is, I am leaving for home and family in one piece while I can.

To Dad, being an assistant pointer would not be a promotion and would create personal concerns for himself. In the day-to-day operations on the mountain, the pointer was responsible for handling all measurements and approving all drilling and blasting to prepare the granite for Gutzon Borglum's final design. The pointer had to constantly lay out new work based on Borglum's scale model so that there would be no delay in using the workmen to the greatest advantage.

Pointing was the term that Gutzon Borglum used to describe the method he and his workers used to transform the raw material, granite, into his subjects, the four presidents. He had developed this technique for himself at Stone Mountain in Georgia as early as 1923. As Rex Alan Smith reports in his book, Borglum discovered that he could "safely adapt blasting to the needs of the sculpture. . . . By drilling lines of holes [in the stone] and loading them with light charges [of dynamite] to be fired simultaneously, [workers] could with one blast remove great sheets of excess stone" (p. 68). Many workers had started their apprenticeship in the role of pointer or assistant pointer; even the sculptor's son, Lincoln Borglum, learned this job. It was dangerous, and the method resulted in much pollution. Great amounts of water in tin cans were brought up the mountain by cable to keep the dust down to protect the workers. Many workers with a mining background had been recruited, so they were accustomed to such unhealthy conditions. They did not complain. Gutzon Borglum paid better wages than the mines did. Years later, reports of serious health issues from damaged lungs among the workers did surface.

Working as an assistant pointer would place Dad on the mountain where the blasting of the rock mass was happening. By this time, over four-hundred-fifty-thousand tons of granite had been blown off the mountain. The dusty and dirty air was not good for anyone's respiratory system. In the back of his mind, Dad still held onto his singing career as a possible alternative to being a sculptor, and the assignment possibility did not please him. It might make it impossible for him to return to the Eastman

School of Music, where he had been studying voice before going to Mount Rushmore.

In his June fourth letter to Mother, Dad expressed his dissatisfaction with the man who had brought him to this place:

Write as soon as you can and please inform me darling what I should do. I cannot waste time, time means a lot to us. If I thought I was learning anything I would stay but G.B. does not work. He has others [do it] then places his name on it, all that is done here. I want the credit. Well, I am surely learning what fakes there are in this world. . . . Darling, at present I don't think it is wise for you to come. I am going to have a long talk with the Borglum[s] and find out all . . . this cannot go on. I have fought and worked hard, they have promised me much but give a little. . . . Here darling they use a man for what they can get out of him. I am sorry we were foolish enough to trust G.B. Now what am I to do—what can I do—although the experience I gained here will be useful.

Dad had come for one main reason: to learn more about sculpting from the master sculptor, Gutzon Borglum. That goal had not materialized. Dad seemed to be testing Mother about the idea of his coming home.

On June 5, Dad provided an update on the accident:

The persons that were hurt here, one is in a very serious condition, the rest seem fair. So here is hoping he gets well soon. They say Happy Anderson has one boy and a wife, and he is a prince of a fellow. But that is the way of a life, no one knows what may happen. Did anything appear in your local papers.

As Dad was expressing his feelings to Mother, events had been unfolding back home in Avon, and Mother was taking matters into her own hands. As the old cliché goes, fate has a sense of humor when dealing with us mortals.

Unbeknownst to Dad, Mother was offered the opportunity to hitch a ride going west on June third. The minister of their church, the Reverend Estes, would be driving to Rockford, Illinois. Knowing of Mom and Dad's separation, he offered her a ride to Rockford, which was as far as he was going. Getting to Rockford would place her somewhere between four and five hundred miles from South Dakota. From there, she would catch a train or bus the rest of the way.

Mother could wait no longer. Missing her husband so intensely, worried about his health, and concerned about the whole family's future, she made a decision. There was no time to debate the pros and cons or to discuss with Dad the timing of such a trip. She just "went for it," deciding to put everything on the line, including leaving her children in the care of family members and friends.

So, on June second, without any advance notice, Mother reported in her diary at 10:30 P.M. that she had made the decision. She would be going to South Dakota, and that would be that. Dad still knew nothing of this latest development. How would he react?

*L*ike an intermission at a performance, the curtain came down on Mother and Dad's love story from June 5 to July 4. I searched through all the letters in the attic trunk and could not find one letter between them during this period.

This gap, I must confess, caused me some concern because it left a huge hole in the story line that I had been following. There was not a single living relative who could tell me what had happened during that time some sixty years ago. Once again, I returned to the attic and searched the trunk, this time taking care to examine items that I had not paid much attention to initially. In a corner, I found more of Mother's diaries.

To my surprise and delight, one of these diaries filled in the missing time period. Then it all became clear to me. There was no correspondence for that month for a good reason: Mother and Dad were together for the first time since Dad's March twenty-seventh departure. I felt elated but also a bit chagrined with myself since the answer had really been so obvious. Even though Mother's entries in this special diary were short, they provided ample information on what had happened during her surprise visit to Mount Rushmore.

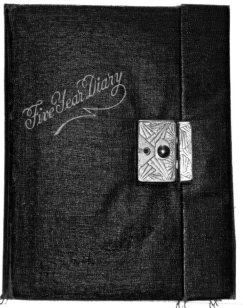

Mother's diary for 1940 is open to April and June entries. Images by Glen Marsh

GREYHOUND Lines
ITINERARY

NAME.. ADDRESS..

FROM.. TO..

CITY	TIME	DAY	TIME	DAY	TIME	DAY	
LV. Rockford, Ill.	6:45PM	1st	Central Line Interstate Transit				Lines
AR. Dixon, Ill	8:00PM	"				"	
LV. "	8:06PM	"				"	
AR. Council Bluff, Ia	6:45AM	2nd				"	
LV. "	9:30AM	"				"	
AR. Sioux Falls S.D.	3:45PM	"				"	
LV. "	10:00AM	3rd	Palace City Lines				
AR. Pierre, S.D.	5:15PM	"	C.T.			"	
LV. "	4:50PM	"	M.T.	Rapid City Lines			
AR. Rapid City S.D.	9:15PM	"	M.T.			"	
LV.							
AR.							
LV. Rockford, Ill.	Union Bus Depot						
AR.	Church & Elm St						
LV.							
AR.							

FARE INFORMATION

ONE WAY FARE FROM.....Rockford Ill...TO...Rapid City S.D. $15.35

ROUND TRIP FARE FROM..........................TO.............................. 27.65

CIRCLE TOUR FARE FROM..........................TO..............................$

The above times are extracts from current schedules and are subject to change without notice. Time of arrival, departure or connection is not guaranteed. Company assumes no liability or responsibility for errors which may occur in the above itinerary.

The bus schedule from Rockford, Illinois, to Rapid City, South Dakota, shows many stops.

On June 4, she wrote:

Mr. Estes and I left Avon at exactly 5 a.m. Eastern D.L.S. time on Route 20 with sandwiches, milk, and fruit juices in a 1932 Plymouth. We talked scatteringly on different subjects, nothing deep or profound on either side. He is easy to get along with, very friendly. It is hard to think of him as a minister.

Her June fifth entry reads, "I left Rockford, Ill., at 3:20 a.m. on the Greyhound bus." Then, on June sixth, she wrote about "the surprise." She called Dad that morning to say that she was on her way and expected to arrive in Rapid City by late evening.

How elated must Dad have been to hear that his sweetheart was on her way to meet him with open arms! I have to believe that this news left my Dad stunned, especially in light of his previous letters telling her not to come. Moreover, he did not react as one would expect or hope, as Mother's diary records: "He acted and talked as though he didn't want me to come to South Dakota, but he was just worried financially, for he had sent me most of his salary the day before."

Finally, on the night of June 6, 1940, Mother arrived in Rapid City, and my parents stayed at the Harney Hotel, a local landmark. I am so grateful that Mother kept track of her experiences in South Dakota and revealed interesting sidelights about Gutzon Borglum and the people she encountered.

JUNE 7
So good to see & be with Art. He was getting quite discouraged here. G. Borglum is temperamental, one minute praising, the next cursing. Art can't take the latter so I'm glad I arrived to philosophize with him. . . . Lincoln Borglum came for us personally in his own car at 1:15 p.m. They gave Art the day

Rapid City in the 1940s. Minnilusa Historical Association at The Journey Museum, Rapid City, S.Dak.

off. Met Mrs. Borglum. She seemed much interested & was very cordial. Mr. G. Borglum spoke & shook hands a couple times. I walked up the mt. to the heads. A wonderful view below.

JUNE 8

Stayed in a cabin in Keystone last night—"Grizzly Camp"—$2.00 & then stayed until 4 p.m.—$.75 more. Modern with toilet and shower. Met Mrs. [Del Bianco] whose husband [Luigi] was assistant sculptor with Borglum for years. She said she had her suitcase packed for years not knowing what minute they would leave. She said that there was no peace or calm for them. Met Mrs. Borglum at Hill City at a dance to-night. Danced with 5 different persons. What a merry crowd! Slept in gov. office quarters to-night. [Dad had been staying in the agent's office since his first day at Mount Rushmore.]

BASEBALL BENEFIT
- **DANCE** -
SPONSORED BY
RUSHMORE ATHLETIC ASSOCIATION
SATURDAY, JUNE 8, 1940
AT
HILL CITY COMMUNITY HALL
ADMISSION $1.00

The first couple of days were sort of a honeymoon period for my parents, but that would not last. On June ninth, Mother wrote: "Frank Skells the Gov. Agent came home for a few minutes so we got up. He was going around with Mrs. McBride, Mr. Borglum's secretary." Frank's schedule had changed, and now he needed his office. He could no longer accommodate my parents.

In fact, they had to be out of there that very night. Going down the mountain to the town of Keystone was not an option. Space was costly and scarce, and they had no car for the commute back and forth. The solution was a tent on the hillside close to Dad's studio. Mother reported in her diary: "Cleaned up tent—what filth. Aired mattress & a couple dirty blankets we have to use." The next day ants were crawling around on their mattress, and yellow jackets flew around the tent. At night, the oil lamp had to be used sparingly because of the bugs it attracted. As for the days, the summer sun of South Dakota made a tent one heck of a hot place to be.

Various entries described the physical conditions: "About 9 our tent is unbearably hot. . . . I take a bath in a pail of water every afternoon. . . . We walk up the hill to the Women's & Men's Rest Room to go to the toilet. . . . bought some spray for the many bugs in our tent." A tent on a cement slab was the extent of their living quarters. In retrospect, however, that kind of "roughing it" would be good training for Mother's future endeavors when, as a seventy-year-old, she joined the Peace Corps and went to southern Thailand.

In spite of hardships, her stay with Dad proved productive for Mother, who had set her own personal agenda, which was to examine the prospects of moving to South Dakota. She wanted the family to be together. In pursuing this goal, she served as a goodwill ambassador for Dad—or perhaps a politician better describes her role.

Mother started by spending a good amount of time making the rounds of the worksite, meeting and greeting the power players— the important people whom she felt might have an influence on her family's future. She seemed fully committed to her belief that Dad's future would best be served if he continued to work with Gutzon Borglum, even if that meant that the entire family would have to pick up and move to South Dakota. The family had to live together. No more two thousand miles of separation. In assessing whether this goal was feasible, she examined every aspect of life on the mountain.

The entries in Mother's diary recorded her spending time with all of the main characters on the Mount Rushmore stage. At the top of the list, of course, were Gutzon Borglum and his wife, Mary, and Lincoln Borglum and his wife, Louella. The remaining

players were quite diverse and included Frank Skells, Mrs. Mc-Bride (identified as Borglum's secretary), the sculptor Luigi Del Bianco, a Mr. Wilcox, Irene Flick (who worked in the restaurant), Bud Linde, Matt Reilly, Ray Berg and his wife, Sylvia, to name some of the people mentioned in the letters and diaries.

While Dad worked long hours in the studio and on the mountain, Mother was active. She noted her observations and concerns in her usual descriptive manner:

JUNE 11

Art works all the time, before work, lunch time, after work, evenings & all in hopes of getting a higher salary. He worked in studio until 9:30 this p.m. & then we went down to Matt's room & talked.

JUNE 12

Art doesn't eat lunch. We pay 1.20 for 4 meals between us per day, not bad. Art gets very discouraged here because of the things

My mother, Mary Grow Cerasani, posed in front of the mountain in June 1940.

that go on. Gutzon Borglum is very temperamental & Art can't take anything but sugar & honey toward him. He works hard & he wants rewards.

JUNE 13

Did our washing this a.m. Had to carry all the water from the kitchen to the tubs. Art emptied them after work. Spent most of the afternoon on the heads on the mt. Watched them drill. This project surely is a big undertaking. Unbearably hot below but up above there was a nice cool breeze. This p.m. Art & I went into Rapid City with Bob. We saw a couple movies.

JUNE 14

Photographers from "Life" Magazine were here taking pictures of the heads. This afternoon Lincoln Borglum took me up on the mt in the bucket. A very thrilling experience. That is the way to view those mammoth heads, approaching them. I took several pictures.

JUNE 15

In the mts it is always cool in the shade & very cool on top of the mt. We never suffer except when we awaken in the a.m. —about 9. . . . We bought sheets.

JUNE 16

Last night we celebrated with sheets on our bed for the first time since we've been in the Black Hills. No longer will I fear germs from dirty blankets even if we did give them a hot sun bath airing. . . . Lots of tourists to-day—1,500 I bet in spite of a hail storm.

Photographers from *Life* magazine talk to Lincoln Borglum (center, facing left) as Gutzon Borglum walks to his car.

JUNE 17

This evening Art & I went over to the ranch with Ray and Sylvia & S's brother. We visited with Lincoln & Louella Borglum. Their home is very unique. Huge living room, unfinished wood, huge fire place, huge lounge, bookcase above. Lincoln very quiet. Fell ill on way home.

Lincoln Borglum, front, and others work in harnesses on Roosevelt's head. Image by Reynor Photo. South Dakota State Historical Society

JUNE 18

Got the curse this A.M. *Felt quite ill all afternoon. Rested for an hr in our terribly hot tent. Read a little. At 4:30 did a washing. Art carried the water for me. Hung the clothes after supper. Art worked at the studio experimenting & then put the heads in oil down at the Bunk House.*

JUNE 19

Bob took Art & me to Rapid City with him this evening.

JUNE 20

Letter from Dad saying everything O.K. at home & to rest here as much as possible. Art is working very hard experimenting. He worked all evening in hot oils & other materials. He has some beautiful finishes on his heads [he was creating models for the tourist trade]. Wrote letters while he worked.

JUNE 21

Gutzon Borglum ate dinner with us at the Bunk House. He asked if Art were born in America. I told him his people came from S.A. [South America] but originally from Italy. He said the better class of Italians went to S.A., the poorer class here where the loot was easier. He called Hitler "Frankenstein." Refused to give his autograph to a boy, for when he asked why he wanted it he said, "I don't know, just for fun, I guess." Borglum said, "Just for fun doesn't mean anything."

JUNE 24

Art fought for $50 a week to-day & Mr. Gutzon Borglum said he should have that much. . . . We went to a movie "Ghost Breakers." Fair.

By the last week in June, Mother had to be pleased with herself. Her diary showed that she had established herself as a guide for tourists on the mountain, making twenty-five cents per person. By so doing, she could help the family if they were to move out west. This entrepreneurial spirit had also served her well when she had gone door to door selling those all-season greeting cards back home.

JUNE 25

Up at 10 a.m. Cleaned out tent. Put blankets on line & sprayed bed, clothes, cracks etc. A very warm day. Terribly hot in the tent. Mr. Borglum talks & it doesn't mean much. L. Borglum said there wasn't enough money left for Art to have $50.00 per week, so I guess I go home next wk without gaining what I came for. Earned $1.75 to-night guiding up the mt.

JUNE 26

We miss Mr. [Del] Bianco. He works on the mt. on Washington's eye as an expert carver at $12.00 per day. He is one of the nicest persons out here. . . . Took 4 up the mt to-night for $1.00.

JUNE 27

This p.m. Art & I, Irene Flick & Marian [Sagdalen], girls who work in the restaurant, drove into Rapid City with Matt [Reilly]. Art & I saw a couple movies & then we went to the carnival. Coffee, the most terrible I ever tasted, cost 10¢ per cup. Hamburgers, cheap & tasteless—25¢ per. Art spent a couple dollars the whole evening.

JUNE 28

Helped Art compose letters to Jones, Hawley & Mrs. Moore. . . . This evening took 2 up the mt. for $.50, up 800 steps. . . . [Art] is

very depressed because I am going home. He says he won't let me, that he won't give me any money.

JUNE 29
Took one up the mt. to-night for $.25.

JUNE 30
Served as guide at Mt. Rushmore all day. Worked alone all a.m. making 4 trips up & down those 800 steps. . . . I stayed up most the afternoon. Art made 2 trips up while I was having dinner & supper. We made $16.00 but believe me, I for one worked hard for it.

JULY 1
July 1st. & the work at Mt. Rushmore still continues & no one seems to know anything definitely. Stayed in bed all morning. My leg muscles are very sore, my head aches & my back hurts, but guess it was worth yesterday's earnings.

JULY 2
Art is acting very depressed because I'm planning to leave. . . . Had a huge chicken dinner to-night with [Marian], Irene, Bob, Matt [Reilly], Mr. [Del] Bianco, Mr. Skells, Art & I. The 8 of us ate 4 chickens. Louella Borglum ate dinner with us this noon.

JULY 3
Mr. Gutzon Borglum posed for pictures for me this a.m. He was very cordial & sent his best wishes to all of my people at home. Lincoln took me on the mt. in the bucket. Matt wouldn't let me go down the faces in the harness. Took my first movie reel. Walked on Washington's shoulder & Lincoln's. Down on scaffolds. Very thrilling! Matt [Reilly] & Art drove me into Rapid City this p.m.

A large dinner bell (the triangle at left) hung on the back corner of the bunk house to call people to meals. Image by Rise Studio. National Park Service, Mount Rushmore National Monument

Nestled into the Black Hills, the Mount Rushmore complex included (1) a machine shop, (2) a compressor house, and (3) the bunk house, where meals were served. Image by Ole A. Vik. South Dakota State Historical Society

By the late 1930s, tourists were frequent visitors at Mount Rushmore. Image by Bell Photo. South Dakota State Historical Society

Workers at the mountain, such as Bud Linde, supplemented their incomes by acting as tour guides. Mother, too, earned some much-needed cash in this way.

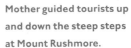

Mother guided tourists up
and down the steep steps
at Mount Rushmore.

As Mother's stay at the mountain
drew to an end, Dad became
depressed as he contemplated
living apart once again.

Saw "My Favorite Wife." Left for Avon, N.Y., from Rapid City at 12:01. Art very sad & me too.

The last part of Mother's entry is reminiscent of that day in March when they first parted at the railroad station in Rochester. Once again, separation was to be their reality.

JULY 4
Art was very depressed because I left him for home, but I'm hoping I can go back. Mr. Gutzon Borglum talked of plans for Art: Working on the new steps, the Hall of Records, and casting on a percentage base.

Borglum's words had to be the most important words she had heard from him. For her, they meant that he had plans for the future, which included Arthur Cerasani. During his stay at Mount Rushmore, Dad had also worked on the model for the granite stairs and the Hall of Records.

JULY 5
Didn't sleep any too well during the night on the bus from Minneapolis to Chicago. Too many stops. Left Chicago at 10:45 a.m. & arrived in Cleveland at 9:30 p.m. I was very sleepy all the way but guess I will be right along. Riding the bus all night, the 3rd night, but will arrive in Buffalo at 4:45 in the morning & in Rochester at 10:10 E.S.T.

Returning home, Mother sent a letter to the Borglums, a draft of which she sent to Dad so he could be informed:

My dear Mr. Borglum,
I again want you to know how much I appreciate being at

July 7, 1940
112 Genesee St.
Avon, N.Y.

Dear Art,

It is 8:30 P.M. The children will be sleeping now so I will try to begin on the 101 events I have to tell you.

The bus rides through S. Dak. were most miserable Wed. night & Thursday. I was ready to resolve to turn in my ticket & come the rest of the way by train. However, the greyhound, which I got on at Watertown was so marvelous in comparison to what I had been riding I decided to continue on them. The journey was so long I just couldn't stay over any place any night & thus arrive home still later & so I arrived home Saturday at 1 P.M. I was in Chicago Friday morning, Cleveland late Friday night and Buffalo, N.Y. at 4:45 Sat. A.M. I waited there until 7:15 & arrived in Rochester at 10:10 Eastern Standard Time. I called your home. Your mother answered & it was very difficult to understand anything. But I did gather the family had gone to Niagara Falls. Fran said they had come here a few days before to get our day bed cushions - the

Mt. Rushmore during June. The great and everlasting tribute to democracy which you so ingeniously have planned and so skillfully are working out leaves me still breathless and full of admiration.

It is my sincere wish and prayer that this great work may continue and that your plans, so beautifully conceived, may be realized. We Americans need something tangible to lift us from our spiritless, restless, mad hankering after a soulless life. The Rushmore Memorial Project has already accomplished this for thousands. I take off my hat to the continuation of such a project.

If Arthur is to stay with you any length of time, I would appreciate knowing the plans. The children and I are very anxious to be near him and would consider living in Rapid City.

Please give my regards to Mrs. Borglum. I wish you both the best of health.

Sincerely yours,
(Mrs. A. J.) Mary Cerasani

hile Mother stayed with Dad on the mountain, they were able to plan their future, share meals, chat with other members of the community, and go to the movies in Rapid City after Dad got off from work. The time after Mother returned home, however, I tend to think of as Dad's "blue period." He must surely have missed her presence and the socializing they had done together.

Mother's diary told of friendships with other workers that had developed during her time on site. Now that she was gone, the emptiness in Dad's life was overwhelming. His letters were full of pathos.

Mount Rushmore
July 4, 1940
Dearest Mary,
Mama, darling, with you my heart has left. I prayed last night that I could be strong, but it was too much for me. My heart was broken and believe me I have never in all my life missed anyone as much as I have you. I see you everywhere and I am waiting to hear your voice, but no my sweetheart is not here. . . .

Mother defended Gutzon Borglum, shown here in his studio with a model, to Dad after her return to New York. "You can't make him over," she wrote, "so accept him as he is, try to do your job well." South Dakota State Historical Society

JULY 5

*I just keep waiting to see you, as you use to walk in while I was
at work, but no Mary. . . .*

In today's vernacular, Mother's response to him could well be
called "tough love," mixed with sage advice.

Avon, N.Y.
July 27, 1940
In Defense of GB
Dear Art,
    *Please try to stand the test. Character is developed only
through hard things. Please try to be intelligent and do the
right thing without a murmur. Get the most you can from your
experience there, and please don't be harping always about GB
etc. You can't make him over so accept him as he is, try to do
your job well and keep your mouth closed about him, please.
Just forget about him unless you have something nice to say.
Art, no doubt, GB is in no position to tell us what he is going to
do about us. His fate rests on uncertainties just as yours does.
It would be just as unreasonable for me to harp on you about
telling me what is to become of us. You don't know, and no doubt
GB doesn't know the same for us. Forget his promises to you.
Think more about the superior kind of work you are going to
do for him. That is your biggest worry. Once you worry enough
about that, the rest will fall [into place] too. Make yourself in
demand. It may take long, steady work, but until you've done
that, stop harping and being so unsettled. Study and read and
try to improve yourself. There should be your worry. I have
written to GB and asked about us. Now it is up to you to prove
yourself and you surely didn't do that while I was at the Mt. You
talked and acted the blubbering fool that has been your downfall*

in past years. You can't fool people, Art. You've got to be able to do something. Unbridled brains and talent mean nothing. . . .

. . . Art, darling, I love you very much and I want so badly for you to be strong. Please try to organize yourself around what exists and not what anyone says or promises. You are old enough to know that words are cheap. You should know too! Act according to existing facts and not what you think ought to be. Be too busy to be always mouthy. That is your great trouble. Learn to listen, to read, to study. You don't have to be the big attraction. You may get that in cheap, common ways, but by so doing, you will never know it honestly for any length of time, for you won't deserve it. You know you are very much like your father. He has to show his authority right or wrong. You have to have attention earned or not earned. I preach, Art, because I love you and I want you to succeed, but you never will until you forget yourself and start developing. It is a long hard process gained not in leaps, but little by little.

Good night, my love. Please try to profit by such words of wisdom. They belong not to me but to those who would be wise.

Mary

In a follow-up letter, Mother wrote:

Somehow or other Art (if you keep your head and your tongue) I feel your future is there. Remember the difficulties of the moment look magnified to the individual while in reality they aren't half as terrible as others have been or might be, and sweetheart, don't get involved in other people's business. It is poor policy and often disastrous . . . confide in NO ONE regardless. . . .

Dad finally seemed to be getting the point when he wrote: "Borglum is being hard on me but I am remaining calm."

(opposite)

Dad, who promised to remain calm while waiting to learn of his future, posed next to President Lincoln's nose.

13 | The World outside Mount Rushmore

One has only to look at the *New York Times* headlines from March to September of 1940 to see what was happening outside of Dad's circumscribed world on the top of Mount Rushmore. By this time, Hitler's German war machine was on the move. Having defeated Poland by the end of September 1939, the Germans looked elsewhere to advance Nazi ambitions. On April 9, 1940, they invaded Denmark and Norway. Then, shortly after dawn on May 10, Nazi Germany launched a massive surprise attack on the Netherlands, Luxembourg, and Belgium. Two days later, Hitler's leading panzer troops began advancing into France. By June 1940, France had fallen. Soon, Nazi bombs would rain down on England.

On the other side of the globe, China was locked in a struggle with an aggressive Japan. By 1940, the Soviet Union had repulsed Japanese attacks and signed a non-aggression pact, but the Soviets were preparing for an inevitable confrontation with Germany. Battles were breaking out all around the world. By almost everyone's description, the world was in a grave situation that deteriorated day by

The New York Times.

VOL. LXXXIX...No. 30,057.   NEW YORK, FRIDAY, MAY 10, 1940.   THREE CENTS NEW YORK CITY | FOUR CENTS Elsewhere Except

NAZIS INVADE HOLLAND, BELGIUM, LUXEMBOURG BY LAND AND AIR; DIKES OPENED; ALLIES RUSH AID

MOUNT RUSHMORE
NATIONAL MEMORIAL COM

May 10, 1940

Dear Mary,

Goodmorning sweetheart, How are you this lovely spring morning? I hope this will not happen again. our first spring apart My life here is very empty darling - you know darling - you are my life, my everything - without you I would not live or care to live How I lived before I meet you I can not believe, but now I know I only lived to meet you, for in you my hope, my everything I dreamed of came to be, you are my inspiration my all. Keep well my darling, dont worry about me, for every act I do I do for us, nothing will I ever do that will shame me, or you, believe me, and love me. You do still love me Mary? I know I am not what you wanted in life. I have been more trouble to you then a help - but you must forgive me and help me. You are wonderful and sweet and a great help. Please buy your self a flower - from me to you and say a prayer for me. Happy mothere day darling If ever God made a beautiful and lovely Mother and a wise one, God made you, Tell Arty and Dickie they are very lucky and should help and protect you and that the mighty God for such a great present. Much love to you Mary darling and tho children, Thanks a million for everything solong darling see you tonight
                                    Always hoping
                                    Arthur
Regards to Dad and love, have him heen well.

On May 10, 1940, Germany attacked the Low Countries and opened a new front in World War II. To Dad, isolated from the outside world on Mount Rushmore, it was just another day, as he wrote home to express his love for my mother. Headline from the *New York Times*, May 10, 1940, © 1940 by the New York Times. All rights reserved. Used by permission and protected by the copyright laws of the United Sates. The printing, copying, redistribution, or retransmission of the content without express written permission is prohibited.

day. Like it or not, the United States was being drawn into these conflicts.

Against this global backdrop, Dad and his co-workers labored on Mount Rushmore. In spite of the numerous dispatches about the intense fighting in Europe and elsewhere, workers on the mountain still lived in relative isolation, receiving news about world events infrequently. Radios were not the common commodity they are today, and while there was at least one on the mountain, there were few if any radios in the men's quarters and certainly not in Dad's tent.

Mother's letters occasionally referred to the world situation, so Dad knew something about the events that were reshaping the world. However, the information was spotty at best and certainly incomplete. Mother wrote:

Dear Art,

Do you see the daily paper to see what a sad mess Europe is in? Tell me, for if you don't I will occasionally send a sheet or so along with my letters. Things are in a deplorable state. I wonder if Germany will get England and France. I suppose that will be where we [the United States] make our grand entry.

The *New York Times* headline on June 1, 1940, made it crystal clear: "Roosevelt Warns War Imperils Whole World." Although Dad did not write many thoughts about the impending war in his letters home, he revealed his philosophical side in notebooks he kept in his studio at Mount Rushmore:

For as this universe spins through space and war destroys lives and treasures, how weak appears man. His ingenuity now blots in one half-hour what thousands of men have sweated years to build! The strength of capital is with us no more when granite and steel lie in ruins. And so the idealist can ask the materialist in these days what he possesses—except his own soul? "The wind blows where it wills and you hear its voice, but know not where it comes from, or where it goes. So is everyone that is born of the Spirit."

The last two sentences, I discovered, came from John 3:8.

Even as these global events were taking place, another type of struggle was occurring on the mountain—the fight for the survival of the Mount Rushmore project and the jobs of its workers.

*a*s world events were spinning out of control, so was Mother's growing concern about the future of Dad's work. She wrote to my father: "Darling, do you think that this terrible war and the recent appropriations for armaments in the country will hinder the project at Mount Rushmore? Be sure to comment on this, dear."

Dad's reply was:

What is new in this great big world? We that live up on this mountain miss the outside world, now when history is in the making, one finds out things after they have happened and almost forgotten. The radio here one can get about 2 stations. The time the news is broadcasted we are working. As for papers we see one a week if we are lucky. So as the world marches on we wait and hope [that] much of the parade does not pass by before we get there.

From the time of Dad's arrival at Mount Rushmore in March 1940, a primary topic of discussion among the workers had been whether or not the four heads of the presidents would ever be fin-

Throughout 1939 and 1940, workers struggled to finish the heads at Rushmore.
Image by Bell Photo. South Dakota State Historical Society

ished. Rumors about Congress cancelling funding for the project led to much speculation and anxiety among the men. My Dad, who was pulled into this rumor mill, worried about his main objective, which was to secure dependable long-term employment so that he could better, or at least maintain, his family's position. He strongly believed that was his role as head of the household. His anxiety about his position began earlier when Frank Skells, the government agent, had confidentially informed Dad that his job might be short-term. On Dad's second day on the mountain, he had told Mother that Skells "likes me and has informed me in confidence to have a heart to heart talk with Mr. Borglum, and has also informed me that the job may last only until June."

At the time, the warning did not overly concern Dad. Now, four months later, the outside world was quite different, and everyone seemed to be aware that the continuation of the work was in jeopardy. Staff and workers were worried. Would they have enough time to finish what Borglum had promised the United States Congress in 1939, when he asked for what he billed as the final appropriation? In January that year, the sculptor had promised that body that he would complete the work in twelve to eighteen months or "by the end of the fiscal year 1940." On April 12, 1940, the local *Rapid City Daily Journal* reminded its readers of that promise, quoting Borglum's testimony before Congress. The newspaper predicted that the statement would "prove troublesome" to Borglum when he asked for more funding.

The workers on the mountain knew that Borglum had always been optimistic when setting time schedules and cost projections, and they also knew that the sculptor was, in fact, having difficulty raising both private and public money to continue the project. After all, the federal government was starting to focus on other issues deemed more important to the nation. The truth of the matter was that there were also politicians who did not share Borglum's vision and dream for Mount Rushmore. They were against it and thought of it as foolish: "What? Carving up a mountain?"

Even tourists visiting and chatting with Dad in the studio had mixed feelings. "Many ask the most foolish questions, and some think G.B. is a joke and a fool," Dad wrote to Mother on May 8. "One person claimed the work isn't so hot, and one could do it and not waste as much money as G.B. is. But that is life, some like and some dislike. Time alone can tell the whole story."

And time had revealed more of the financial situation. In his letter of April 17, Dad reported the financial status directly from the source: "Yes, GB did tell me he needed more money, without it the whole work will fold up." By April 22, the picture was becoming more gloomy as Dad realized "how uncertain the job is here—we are in hopes, that is all of us, that the job goes on, if it stops we all will be seeking our fortunes elsewhere." Then on April 27, he wrote: "I won't know until after July how permanent this job really is."

Unlike my Dad, many of the workers had been with Gutzon Borglum since the inception of the work in 1927. At that time, a labor pool of stone carvers was not available in this country; they were to be found in Europe. For the most part, Borglum had taken unskilled construction workers and miners and taught them the skills he required. The workers had had relatively steady employment throughout the period of the Great Depression. Now, during the summer of 1940, the workplace conversation was all about "GB running out of money" and whether there would be any new appropriations from Washington.

As the fiscal year drew to a close, the news was that Gutzon Borglum was heading to Washington in an attempt to get Con-

Gutzon Borglum, charismatic artist, was not always a successful businessman or effective fundraiser. South Dakota State Historical Society

gress to loosen the purse strings once again. The brilliant, charismatic artist who had conceived Mount Rushmore was on a "Beg for Bucks" trip to the nation's capital.

On July 26, Dad painted a bleak picture of events on the mountain. "GB made a statement that this week will be the end," he wrote. So far, my Dad's love letters home had revealed all the "chatter," both good and bad, that was going around the mountain. Often, it was merely rumor or speculation, but it produced anxiety and uncertainty. Would the work go forward or come to a grinding halt?

From Dad's letters home, it seems obvious that he and his fellow workers were not preoccupied with world events. Mother's letters, on the other hand, reveal a great deal of anxiety over the topic of war and the dangers that Dad's Italian background posed for him. Mother's concern about Dad's ethnicity reached all the way back to their courtship days. Mussolini had invaded Ethiopia in October 1935, and as a result, Italians had gotten a lot of attention in the news, and it was far from good attention. Dad's letter to Mother dated May 19, 1936, certainly indicated his awareness of Mussolini's growing involvement in world affairs: "Last night my sister, brother and little me went to the theatre to hear Mussolini talk [newsreel footage] and we also saw *After the Night of Love*—the two pictures were marvelous."

Bad publicity for Italians in the United States reached a peak on May 22, 1939, when Mussolini announced to the world that he was joining forces with Adolf Hitler in the Pact of Friendship and Alliance, more commonly referred to as the Pact of Steel. By taking this action, the Italian leader antagonized the American public, and a wall of suspicion quickly arose around Italians living in America.

In the middle of Dad's residency at Mount Rushmore—June 28, 1940, to be exact—Congress passed and the president signed legislation that significantly curtailed the rights of Italian Americans and Italian aliens. With the support of President Franklin D. Roosevelt and FBI director J. Edgar Hoover, Congress passed the Alien Registration Act, as the news media fed a growing national paranoia toward Italians living in the United States and Canada.

With the local newspaper reporting that hundreds of Italians had been arrested in Canada, Mother could not have been isolated from the news of the day as Dad was. After all, the Canadian border was less than two hundred miles from Avon, New York. The May 16, 1940, *New York Times* headline read, "Roosevelt Again Calls on Italy to Keep Out." Less than a month later, on June 11, the *Times* reported, "Italy at War, Ready to Attack; Stab in Back, Says Roosevelt; Government Has Left Paris." Although the *New York Times* was not readily available to Mother, the *Democrat and Chronicle* of Rochester, New York, confirmed her worst fears. On June 11, its headlines shouted, "French Government Flees; Italy Enters War Today."

After President Roosevelt gave a speech that referred to Italy's entrance into the war, Mother's speculations of what could happen here in the States seemed well grounded. Her letters took on the additional mission of protecting Dad from the harmful effects of his Italian background and of his talking about it:

Be brave, darling, and be wise. Watch that tongue. Should we get into war, it is going to be hard on all Germans and Italians especially those of 1 generation back. The least thing will be

Adolf Hitler, center left, and Benito Mussolini, shown here in Venice in 1934, joined forces in the Pact of Steel in 1939. Image by Istituto Nazionale Luce. Library of Congress

President Franklin D. Roosevelt speaks here on September 27, 1940, the day that the Tripartite Pact between Japan, Germany, and Italy was signed. Franklin D. Roosevelt Library, Hyde Park, N.Y.

held against you—so think twice for the sake of Arty Jr., Dick
& me if for nothing else. In Canada, Germans and Italians are
in concentration camps or something of that sort. They won't
take chances for these are spies & sympathizers—so hold your
tongue. England will win or we will be in the war. Please keep
a level head & let your head not your heart rule. You are an
American. So am I. Let's not have it sound otherwise. Let your
sympathies also be with home deals.

JULY 11
Darling avoid talk about yourself and your past regardless
of how good a friend you think anyone is. And above all stop
trying to defend people in this country. If they can't defend
themselves they aren't worth much and the letter goes for many
of them. You defend them constantly and you will be classed
with them. Heaven forbid! Please take the advice of looking on
objectively. They just don't deserve it, Art, and it only does you
harm.

Her warnings continued throughout the summer, as in her letter of August 22:

You should have heard [your sister] Clotilda and me
discussing the war situation! You know how huffy she talks.
Well, we both talked in huffs—she against England at any cost,
and I against the Hitler type of rule at any cost. I would rather
see England than Hitler win even should we have to go to war
for, I maintain, with all England's faults and mistakes, her
domination is a far better type than Hitler's pagan, immoral
tyrannical rule which usurps the morals and blood of a nation
for his own embellished power. Well, you should have heard us.
I guess your mother was worried for fear we were fighting and

tried to stop us. We assured her we were just putting down our
points emphatically but in a friendly attitude.

Mother was obviously trying to send Dad a message to think twice about his formerly positive attitude toward Mussolini, who had now allied himself with the Third Reich. She believed his sister was already "far gone." Mother could not let that happen to her husband.

16 | The Faust Temptation

Mother had recorded in her bridal book that on February 7, 1936, "Arthur placed the engagement ring on my finger in the New York Central R. R. Station, Rochester, N.Y., about midnight. I had just heard *Faust* at the Eastman Theater."

Readers will likely recall the story of Faust in the classic works of Marlowe and Goethe. Faust sells his soul to the devil in exchange for worldly pleasures. *Good grief,* some reader might be thinking, *what connection can there be between Faust and the love letters from Mount Rushmore?*

A link between the two came about almost by accident. Faust and my father were both tempted. In his letter of May 18, Dad had alluded to a test:

> *Good morning Mary darling. How are you this morning? Did you sleep well? Do you ever dream of your papa so far away? Do you miss me as much as ever? I do. Well darling isn't this the test you were asking for. If my love for you isn't proven by my stay here, then God has never made a heavenly love—and I am a fool. Remember how you use to say that I loved you only when I was near you, well what do you think now. One must*

be tempted in order to find out if he can take temptation. Now is the test, I have many ways—if I wanted them—to forget my loneliness and difficulties. And I thank God, for he has given me a mind, soul and body—which I shall never disgrace. I am a friend of man—but for his vice no—I don't believe in them. I may smile, but my heart shall always be cold, for it does not belong to me—and you have it—the only warmer it ever gets—is when you, and you alone magnetize it, please believe me Mary. I would not say all this, but I do remember what you use to tell me, I hope you realize that I am one in a million. Modest fellow I say. If you do come darling, buy some beautiful clothes and have your hair curled, like you had when you came home from the south, remember when I first met you. Much love to you and the children.

On August 5, after Mother had left South Dakota, Dad returned to the theme of temptation:

Well darling here it is Monday and I am still busy working with [Hugo] Villa. . . . Villa today asked me if I had a good time with some of these girls—he claims they like me. When I told him how I felt about that subject, he was surprised and pleased, he said that there are few persons like me, and also said you must have a fine woman for a wife to respect her so. And I have said I [have] the best in all the world. He is quite a ladies man although he has two grown up girls and a wife. The wife is not what he wanted, he is a good musician and what he likes she does not. But I have one that is real and marvelous and I love her very much.

In two more letters, Dad further described the strength of his fidelity:

Among the Mount Rushmore staff and families were many attractive women. Dad is shown here with a group that included Marian Sagdalen and Louise Wilcox.

They all think I am a fool and they claim they have never seen a man act the way I do, as strong and young and not fall. I have ideas and principles and will always keep them high because I have a wife that I respect, love and worship. As I do believe others will too. Lib and the others do what they want. I shall do what I think is best for me regardless of what they say or think. Much love to you my darling and to my darling children. . . .

. . . The men try real hard to make me forget I am married and to carry on as they do. Villa and all the rest are the same. Women are the only thing they have on their mind and what they can get from them. But I am still true to my darling and will always be. I hope you think of that and forgive me for some of my faults—which I have none. Ha, ha, ha.

Dear Mary,

Good morning sweetheart. How are you darling? How are my darling children? Are they better? How about the fever? Please be careful Mary they are so small and need protection.

No letter yesterday, but there is nothing one can do but wait. I am so sick of being away from you and the children. This being separated isn't what I call the best thing. By the looks of things we will be this way a long time. I wish we could plan and had something to plan with, but at present nothing.

Darling you are going to have your picture and Arty's taken and send it to me—it means so much to me please. I really mean it when I said I will stop writing, so please hurry.

It's very cold here this morning, but I'll get use to it. I love the great open spaces anyway so you see I am going native. The [people] here make one sick, there ideals and habits, but they cannot break me down. I have so much it makes me feel sorry

Dad filled his spare time with activities such as panning for gold in the Black Hills.

for the fools—the best wife in the world plus two sweet loveable children. No hardship is too great for me. So worry not, your husband loves and respects you and will always. I will never do anything that will make you lose respect or love for me, for if that would ever happen, there would be nothing to live for. I love you and miss you darling. Much love to the children.

*   Always yours forever,*
*   Arthur*

Unlike Faust, my father did not yield to the temptation to which it would have been so easy for him to fall prey. What had kept him so faithful to my mother? In my opinion it was something that Princess Buttercup in the movie *The Princess Bride* would fully understand: true love.

Dad was certainly no Willy Loman, the character who yielded in playwright Arthur Miller's *Death of a Salesman*. Mother had to have been pleased. The Faust factor was not in play, in spite of the separation that greatly tested their love. These letters are surely a monumental tribute to the power of true love.

*a*s July 1940 drew to a close, no one had a clear sense about the fate of the Mount Rushmore project. Would Gutzon Borglum's work be finished or not? Information and misinformation abounded as daily rumors floated about. As Dad reported, "It's hard to know what is going to happen here, one hears so many stories." Dad's letters reflected the prevailing sense of chaos and frustration.

JULY 16

He [Gutzon Borglum] really is getting harder to get along with. But I am carrying on just for you and the boys. Now he has me helping move heavy logs and steel down in the basement of the new studio. He claims I am getting too fat and need the exercise.

JULY 19

G.B. seems to pick on me. If I am away for one minute he asks, "Where is Arthur?" Now he claims I am getting fat. "That will never do Arthur; I'll have to give you some hard work." So now my darling I am painting the insides of the new studio. Now how do you like that for nerve Mary!? I'll have to take it and like it for your sake and the children.

Well, Mary, it's the same old grind, even worse. I do hope there is a change before long or I'll burst. . . . LB is still away and GB is riding me, but I can take it, you bet I can.

By July 26, Dad's overall view of events at the mountain had deteriorated, and the stress was obviously taking its toll on everyone:

G.B. made a statement that this week will be the end, there is no more money and nothing is coming. I think Wed. will be the last day of work and if the money does not come we are closing the works for about 5 months. G.B. is going to Washington—so here is hoping things happen.

This week is surely a honey—fights everywhere, everybody seems unhappy. Matt and I seem like angels, trying to help people in distress. Mrs. McBride quit and wanted me to— it's a long story. Frank is sad and crying. His children left yesterday—Jean fought with Mrs. G.B. [and] Ray and Sylvia fought and were going to leave one another.

This seems like a real hell.

Finally, the news that everyone had dreaded was announced. Dad explained it to Mother as fully as he could:

Well the news is here, Wednesday July 31st, we shut down. GB is going to Washington Sunday. In about a week after he arrives in Washington, we will know for how long we will be closed. I don't know as yet what plans I am to make. No funds, claims GB, now this. But I will wait and see what I can do or what will be done. I am sorry about this but what can we do about it, we are helpless.

Mother sent this picture of Artie and me to Dad after her return to Avon.

the Final Days | 157

During July, Dad painted the inside of the new studio, which sits below the heads on the mountain. He resented another assignment that did not use his artistic talent. South Dakota State Historical Society

Luigi Del Bianco and Dad, along with Hugo Villa, who is not shown, worked on the large model of Rushmore.

As the work came to a halt and everyone's fortunes were set adrift, morale reached its lowest ebb, but a new Arthur J. Cerasani was emerging. His mood and his fortunes seemed to be going against the prevailing winds.

JULY 28

No word from Washington.... Now I am working with a super sculptor. The man that has been doing most of GB's work and what a man he is. I saw some of his work and GB cannot hold a candle to him. He is Hugo Villa, a real artist. All morning I have been working with him. He indeed seems to be the master I have been looking for. No news as yet. The only thing so far is that GB left for Washington this morning.

JULY 30

The mountain closed last night. No one is working here but Villa, Bianco, and Cerasani.... I am working with Villa on the large model, he likes my work and for once since I came here I am happy. I am working harder than I ever did, but it's wonderful. He is a master and just as nice as Bianco. I pray we three can always work together.

JULY 31

This is the second day the mountain is closed. I have been working at the studio with Villa. I think tonight is the last day. Then we might work until Saturday but we know that the time is drawing near for us too.

AUGUST 2

At present, no one knows the outcome. I believe the mountain will be closed for a long time. As for other jobs here, there are

LUIGI DEL BIANCO 1892–1967

Luigi Del Bianco was born May 8, 1892, outside Le Havre, France, during his parent's return journey from the United States to Italy. As a small boy, he spent time around his father's wood-carving shop. Recognizing his son's interest and greater-than-ordinary ability, his father sent Del Bianco to Venice to study under an accomplished stone carver. He headed for America when he was seventeen after his cousins in Vermont wrote him that skilled carvers were needed. He returned to Europe to fight for Italy during World War I and settled in Port Chester, New York, once the war was over.

Luigi Del Bianco started working for Gutzon Borglum at his studio in Stamford, Connecticut, and the association between the two men continued until Borglum's death. In 1933, Borglum hired Del Bianco to be the chief stone carver on the Mount Rushmore National Memorial. He held this position until 1940, when money for the project ran out.

On June 26, 1940, Mary Cerasani wrote in her diary: "We miss Mr. Bianco. He works on the mountain on Washington's eye as an expert carver at $12 per day. He is one of the nicest persons out here." Del Bianco was a charismatic figure endowed with a great sense of humor. He was a practical joker and a "ladies' man." Arthur Cerasani told many stories about the sculptor and expressed his sincere fondness for the man.

Luigi Del Bianco passed away on January 20, 1967.

none. I can really call myself a sculptor now. I am doing most of the modeling now. Villa is a great person and for the last three days his back ached so I am trying to do most of the work. He likes my work and we get along like sweethearts. . . . But I want to carry on [with] this type of work. It's real. . . . I am trying to sell myself to Villa. He is from Texas and a great sculptor. This my dear will be my life work.

AUGUST 3
The place is as silent as a tomb. There is only one man working on the faces and that is Bianco. I am still working with Villa. Its hard work but I like it. I am trying to study when the boys are not trying to make me drunk. I am drinking every night, and can I take it.

AUGUST 5
Well, darling, here it is Monday and I am still busy working with Villa. I like my work very much. I pray I may work for a long time with Villa, he is the tops as an artist and a friend.

As I was reading Dad's August letters, I felt as if I were in some sort of a "twilight zone." It was so strange to know about all that was going on in the world in 1940 and how bad things were, while at the same time my Dad was finally experiencing the happiness and career advancement that he had been searching for when he first set out on his journey to South Dakota.

For me, some of the letters conjured up images of Marlon Brando from the movie *On the Waterfront.* He would show up at the shipping docks looking for work every day, only to find out there was no work for him. In his letter of August 7, Dad wrote, "The men come every day. That is, a few of them to find out if we will start." Sadly, they were turned away.

When Dad started working on the Hall of Records, the project was far from finished, giving him hope for future employment.

AUGUST 8

We are still working at the studio and still no definite word from Washington.

AUGUST 9

Today Villa and I started the entrance to the Hall of Records. It was hot and the studio was full of tourists asking this and that. . . . My work now is pleasant and I like it.

AUGUST 11

We are just hoping and waiting. Most of the men are here daily asking when do we start. It's very difficult to do anything here. There are very few places one can get a job and all the jobs have been taken.

AUGUST 13

LB was away for a long time. He returned for about 5 days and now has gone away again. He has not been here for a week. Matt is planning on leaving tonight or the next day. Most of the boys are still hanging around for news so as they may make their plans.

AUGUST 15

It's hard to say at present what I think, you see Mary I don't know if we will be here another two months. . . . We are expecting GB any day now. LB is away at present and Matt was away yesterday morning.

AUGUST 16

No news as of yet, all seems to be quiet on the western front. How are you and the children? Are they well and happy? . . . The tourists are falling off, not so many but they still come.

Lincoln Borglum, center, and Matt Reilly, right, along with James LaRue, left, played prominent roles in the carving of Mount Rushmore. Image by Bert Bell. National Park Service, Mount Rushmore National Monument

Do you miss me, Mary? I do miss you and how. Last night I could not sleep and of late I have not felt right. I worry about you and the children. . . . Darling, how I long for you, to hold you close to my heart, to hear your soft voice.

AUGUST 17

Yes, I am still in the new studio working on the Hall of Records with Villa. We are now making and finishing the entrance. I believe I am still paid by the Government.

NOTICE

NO[...]ASSING
THIS [...]ES TO ALL
VISITO[...] ATTENDED
BY GUID[...]OUNTAIN
TOP. G[...] FOUR
OR LE[...]Y
GUID[...]VE
CENT[...]TIES
EXCE[...]
NUM[...]NGE
WITH[...]AL
ATTE[...]
BE S[...]
CHIL[...]
TO [...]

In August, Dad gained
additional income by
doing a little tour guiding.

AUGUST 18

*I am very tired today and quite sunburned. I did a little guiding
and made a few dollars so as to keep the wolf off my front door.
Mr. GB is here and I just saw him long enough to say hello. He
seems quite well and hardy. He was up on the mountain for*

about ½ hour, he, LB and a photo man. They took pictures and then departed.

AUGUST 22
I am still working on the Hall of Records. This model is quite large. There is the entrance and the room. The room alone is 2 inches to the foot. It's 100 by 80 by 34, so it's no fun. But we are here to work and work we will.

AUGUST 23
Today GB talked to a group of girls up at the old studio. After he was through he brought them down to the new studio and made me talk to them. GB has really been fine these few days. He also gave me a check that was due me for all the work I did on the heads. I have been working hard that is why sometimes I don't write. . . . It's hard grind all day but it's worth it and pray that it might continue.

AUGUST 26
Well darling the mountain once more is closed and no work until further notice. I am sorry I couldn't send the type of news we both are praying for. So here is hoping we get some money in a hurry because without money we cannot work.

AUGUST 28
Mary about my asking GB, it's foolish. First thing he does not know, no one really knows until Uncle Sam gives. If he does I will work. . . . Please believe me this is really a hell here. LB does not know [either]. . . . As for the future, God only knows. Mr. G. Borglum is a very sick man mama and has not been near the mountain for about a week.

HUGO VILLA 1880s–1948

Hugo Villa was born in the mid-1880s in northern Italy. He initially emigrated to Mexico, but by 1918, he was in the United States. In the 1920s, he lived in New York and Washington, D.C., and worked as both a violin maker and a sculptor. He assisted Gutzon Borglum with two important projects, the *Wars of America* installation in Newark, New Jersey, and the monument to the Confederacy at Stone Mountain. By the end of the decade, Villa had his own studio in San Antonio, Texas.

When Gutzon Borglum began his work on Mount Rushmore, he again turned to Hugo Villa for assistance. A conflict over the terms of his employment and problems in the carving of Jefferson's head resulted in Villa's departure in 1931, but his skill as a carver and his underlying friendship with Borglum brought him back to the mountain by the mid-1930s. Arthur Cerasani held Villa's art in the highest regard; on July 28, 1940, he wrote to his wife: "Now, I am working with a super sculptor. The man that has been doing most of G.B.'s work and what a man he is. I saw some of his work, and G.B. can't hold a candle to him. He is Hugo Villa, a real artist!"

After the work at Mount Rushmore ended, Villa returned to Texas, where he continued to work as a sculptor. He died in San Antonio on November 4, 1948.

AUGUST 30

I may surprise you and come home any day now. We are on our last dollar. There are a few of us lucky ones left. . . . The mountain has been closed again since last Saturday, so you see Mary it really would be foolish for you to start coming out. . . . There is no one here that can make an honest statement concerning what is going to happen. Villa thinks Saturday may be our last working day, so I am in a swell fix. . . . Last night Villa and the boys gave me a birthday party. We all had a good time but my thoughts were with you all day thinking and loving you and praying we were together.

SEPTEMBER 3

Well Mary, I am alone now. This evening, not a soul in sight. It's a good thing I took Matt's radio and have it in my tent so I have music as a friend. Gee! Mary it's lonesome out here and I miss you very, very much. Mary, I am working but do not know from day to day when the end will come so you see I have been lucky. . . . No news for you yet darling, everything is about the same. The tourists are falling away fast so this place will almost be like a haunted place. I am experimenting and modeling with Villa. I keep very busy most of the time so I don't have time to worry. Good night darling, see you in my dreams.

SEPTEMBER 5

Dear Mary,

I'm sorry you feel that I am not sending you much information but I have none to give. As I told you before, I am lucky I have been working this long, but it's almost over now. I was talking with LB and he told me we have enough money for about 10 to 12 days. After that if no money comes we are closing for good and I will return to you darling. It's been very hard here. Please don't make it harder for me Mary by claiming I am beating around the bush. I now am sorry I did not have you come from the first but now it's too late. We would have been together and left together.

If this place closes I hope I can find a job with Villa in Texas. God what are we to do if this does close Mary? In your letter you talk as if I did not miss you or love you. You know Mary I miss you and need you very much. It's really not living without you but it's my cross and I'll have to take it. . . . You and only you can make me live and really feel like a human instead of a machine. Please darling love me, write it, you are all I want in this world. You are all I see and think of. No one matters. Please be kind and think kindly of me. . . . I suffer more for I am alone and have no one to love—the children are with you. I have you in my heart and live in the past. I see you over and over loving, smiling, holding me whispering to me.

Always,
Arthur

SEPTEMBER 10

Well mama darling here is some news for you. Frank returned to find we have no more money. I get gipped out of my vacation plus maybe my salary for this payroll. If all the money is gone we have been working for nothing. Now, what a fine mess this is. What can be done? No one knows. Frank is sending a letter to find out so I will work and wait hoping. Mary shall I wait a week or two to find out if more money is coming or shall I come home? We are waiting for congress. LB and GB they are in the dark now. . . . I must have my birth certificate. Mary, do you want me to go south and work at the Panama Canal? They say they need men. Or enroll for war service?—we must live some way.

SEPTEMBER 11

Things are dying fast here. We are in hopes something may happen but it's almost impossible so before you may know it I'll be home again to you for the winter. It's been very cold out here for the last three days and the nights are colder with heavy winds blowing. I wish you were here to keep me warm Mary darling.

Across the mountain, things were shutting down. It was September, so the weather was changing. The tourists were gone, and the lack of activity made the surroundings look more like the Old West ghost towns we have seen in pictures and films. Dad wrote: "I am cold in my tent. It really froze last night and I was cold oh boy and nights are colder with heavy winds blowing. The days are turning grey . . . things are dying fast here."

SEPTEMBER 12

In the art line, it's hard to say [what] you are going to do. The Texas plan has not worked out as Villa planned but if it does he is sending for me to work with him. As for working here, there is no hope. GB has no money of his own and he is losing all, . . . so that side is off too. We are not working at present and are waiting for the payroll. Frank telephoned Washington if they could O.K. enough money for this payroll which they kindly did O.K., so we are sure of about 10 days' pay. I must wait for the 20th to receive my pay.

SEPTEMBER 13

No news from Washington. . . . It's really looking like a ghost town. . . . I am very sorry that we cannot go on with the work out here due to lack of funds. But if GB is in charge I shall return some day, maybe in the spring.

SEPTEMBER 14

No life is left here, it's becoming colder and the old wind does surely blow. Our tourists have disappeared too, so what is there left? . . . Villa is starting to pack and promises me he will send for me as soon as he needs me, not bad hey mama? This art game is indeed hard but there is a lot to it, so here is hoping.

SEPTEMBER 15

Well here we are at beautiful Mount Rushmore doing nothing but waiting. . . . We will do a little finishing and retouching on our own time. They say Congress closes shop the 1st of October. I don't know at present if I will wait that long but I believe not. So Mary darling, if soon no words come from Washington, I will be seeing you. Now I'll try to come part way with Bianco—that should be a great savings. As I figure it, it will be all but 400 miles. I am going to ship some clay home soon and my books then I shall ship myself. I am in hopes that something happens the last minute. . . . Most of the men on the mountain have gone to other states for jobs. So at present, things don't seem so rosy. At present vacationing at Rushmore are Villa, Bianco, Matt, Frank, and Arthur. That is all.

SEPTEMBER 17

We are not working at present for money but we are trying to finish the Hall of Records. GB thanks us very much for helping but as for money he cannot pay us. Before I come home Villa is taking me around the hills. Villa is surely a great person and very likeable. . . . Sorry things did not turn out so that we could all be together here but it still may happen some time this spring. . . . So long darling, I love you very much.

At top, sculptor Hugo Villa works on the mountain with Gutzon Borglum, center. Villa himself signed the photograph. National Park Service, Mount Rushmore National Monument

In examining the last few words of the September eighteenth letter, I felt there was a bittersweet ending to the play. The work at Mount Rushmore was not everything Dad had thought it would be, but by the end, he was able to experience true fulfillment. Now he would be going home to the woman he loved and the children he so missed.

Dad's last letter from Mount Rushmore ended as true as his first. His exiting line: "I cannot wait to come home. I am so lonesome for you my darling sweetheart, I cannot wait to hold you in my arms—until then, goodnight and sweet dreams, darling love. Love you, love and more love. Always Arthur."

With this last closing, the curtain slowly descends with no players left for the audience to applaud. The love letters between Mother and Dad came to an end on September 18, 1940. As is typical at the end of any play, the actors went in different directions, seeking work elsewhere. Hugo Villa went to Texas; Luigi Del Bianco settled in Port Chester, New York; and Arthur J. Cerasani went home to his family in Avon, New York.

18 | *Life after Mount Rushmore*

On September fifteenth, Mother wrote her last love letter to Dad at Mount Rushmore. It gives us a good inkling of what awaited him on his arrival home.

> *112 Genesee St.*
> *Avon, N.Y.*
> *Sept. 15, 1940*
> *Dear Art,*
> *Another nice day, but it is raining outside and the patter makes me all the more lonely in this house by myself.*
> *Arty is always talking about the Mt. closing down, and the Mt. being so far away, and Poppy coming home, and he likes Poppy better than me. Today he said there was a fire at the Mt. and maybe his Poppy would get burned. He stressed the maybe. It all comes from a clear sky and he seems so logical in this thinking. Dick still insists on kissing your picture many times a day.*
> *I have been watching the paper for singles for rent. Some just outside of Rochester are as low as $18 per mo. —a 3 room house for $18, a 4 room one for $23 and one for $27. Of course I don't like*

the environment, but it sounded O.K. and some of the houses are new and have lots with them which would be fine. If you come home and are able to get work, which I'm sure you can, of some sort, I hope there still will be something of the sort available. A lot is more important than extra rooms, for the children need space for playing. Everyone remarks about them, "What healthy looking specimens"—and I always think, Thanks to this big place and lots of lawn and fresh air and sunshine. They have had plenty of all that this summer. Arty has improved 100%. Dick has developed tremendously. . . .

. . . I am going to enclose a snap of Artie. It is all I have so please return it right away. Show it to Mrs. Wilcox and others I know there and then send it back. I'm trusting you to do this so don't fail me, please.

Good luck darling. You may even be on your way home now.
Love,
Mary

Five days passed before the speculation and uncertainty that had surrounded my parents' life came to an end. With the arrival of a telegram on September 23, 1940, a new dawn was approaching. In her diary entry that day, Mother wrote:

Art to arrive tonight at 6:30 E.S.T. Lib drove me into Rochester at 3 p.m. I bought a pair of shoes. Train on time. Art is tanned much. Gee it is wonderful having him home with us. The children knew him though he has been gone 6 months. Arty was all laughs and talk. Logical, intelligent talk.

September 23, 1940, truly was a day of celebration for our family. Our Dad was home, and everyone was happy. Dad immediately started doing things around the house. He went out and bought toys for us boys and porterhouse steaks and the best lamb chops available. I remember when I was growing up, we always had the best food my parents' money could buy and plenty of it. That certainly was the Italian way. Meals were the center of everything. The Cerasani clan loved eating and sharing with others. At supper time Dad cooked often, and there was plenty of food for anyone that happened to stop by, be it lunch or supper. *"Mangia, mangia"* (Eat, eat) was the mantra.

I believe that the best and most fortuitous news of all came from Mother's diary the next day, September 24, 1940: "Tonight Art teaches evening school at Monroe High. Last week Mr. Jones was anxious about him and wanted him. He arrived just in time."

This piece of information is phenomenal for a couple of reasons. One, of course, is that Dad had a job waiting for him when he got back to Avon. Even more extraordinary, it was a job as an artist. For an artist, whether an actor, singer, dancer, musician, painter, or sculptor, going from one job to the next in such a short period of time is just incredibly lucky and falls into the miracle category. I know this from my own career as an actor and earning my livelihood from my passion. An artist can go for months and months without work in his chosen field. In between jobs, unemployment stories are legendary and notoriously long.

With this new job, Dad began teaching art in schools under adult-education programs. Over the years, the assignments evolved, and my Dad became one of the pioneers in the use of art as therapy for people in institutions such as hospitals and homes for the aged. Dad's record of success in this field was outstanding. Many newspaper articles and letters I found in the attic attest to his achievements.

During the fall of 1940, Dad maintained contact with the Borglums and some of the workers. It was his way of keeping informed about what was happening at the mountain, and Dad's hope of returning to work on Mount Rushmore remained front

This picture of the
reunited Cerasani family
was taken in June 1941.

and center for a good six months. Only three men had been left standing during those final days on the mountain, and he had been one of them. That fact gave Dad a great sense of satisfaction and fed his hope that when Washington appropriated more money he would be called in to work again.

Also, Gutzon Borglum had expressed his gratitude to Villa, Bianco, and my father for their continued dedication even after the money had dried up. During that time, the three of them had been working on the models of the Hall of Records and the stairways. This work, which represented the next stage in Gutzon Borglum's plan, had already been provided for by Washington in the Rushmore Bill of 1938. The Hall of Records was to serve as the resting place for America's treasures, which would chronicle the story of our country and serve as the showcase for future generations.

Then, on March 6, 1941, about five and a half months after Dad's departure from Mount Rushmore, his expectations changed dramatically—*again*. Mother's diary recorded the event:

Mr. Borglum died early this a.m., leaving his son Lincoln to carry on for him the Rushmore Memorial project in South Dakota where Art worked for 6 months last year. Reporters called for Art's story of his association with Mr. Borglum.

The newspapers reported that Gutzon Borglum had been on his way to Washington to request funds for the continuation of his work on Mount Rushmore. Apparently he had first stopped off in Chicago to check with his doctor regarding some health issues. On February seventeenth, the sculptor had undergone surgery for a prostate problem that had previously existed. The surgery had apparently gone well, but the sculptor developed a blood clot, and then on March 6, he suddenly died from an em-

bolism. Gutzon Borglum, the talented and charismatic artist, was gone. Dad sent his condolences to the Borglums, receiving a reply from Lincoln:

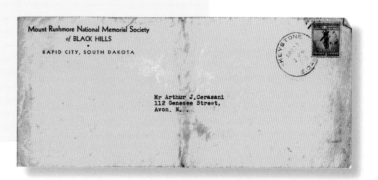

**MOUNT RUSHMORE
NATIONAL MEMORIAL COMMISSION**

COMMISSION
William McReynolds, Chairman
W. J. Bulow, Vice Chairman
Russell Arundel, Secretary
George W. Norris   L. B. Hanna
John Townsend   Isabella Greenway King
Kent Keller   Lorine J. Spoonts
E. F. McDonald, Jr.   William Williamson
George Philip

Gutzon Borglum, Sculptor-Director
Doane Robinson, Historian
Lincoln Borglum, Superintendent

EXECUTIVE OFFICES
Mount Rushmore
Keystone, South Dakota
◆

EXECUTIVE COMMITTEE
Kent Keller, Chairman
E. F. McDonald, Jr., Vice Chairman
Russell Arundel, Secretary
W. J. Bulow   William Williamson
William McReynolds, Ex-Officio

COMMITTEE ON DESIGN AND PUBLICITY
Gutzon Borglum, Chairman
W. J. Bulow   George Philip
E. F. McDonald, Jr.   Lorine J. Spoonts
William McReynolds, Ex-Officio

April 22nd 1941.

Dear Arthur:

It was very kind of you to write, and I regret not being more prompt in answering.

I know that you realize more than most people the loss that we have all suffered, since you have had the opportunity of working with my father.

I sincerely hope that things are going well with you.

Please remember me to Mary.

Sincerely,

Lincoln

To Arthur J. Cerasani
Avon. N.Y.

Mount Rushmore National Memorial Society
of BLACK HILLS
•
RAPID CITY, SOUTH DAKOTA

Mr Arthur J. Cerasani
112 Genesee Street,
Avon. N.Y.

Dad received this letter from Lincoln Borglum in the fall of 1941.

MOUNT RUSHMORE
NATIONAL MEMORIAL COMMISSION

COMMISSION
William McReynolds, Chairman
W. J. Bulow, Vice Chairman
Russell Arundel, Secretary
George W. Norris   L. B. Hanna
John Townsend   Isabella Greenway King
Kent Keller   Lorine J. Spoonts
E. F. McDonald, Jr.   William Williamson
George Philip

Gutzon Borglum, Sculptor-Director
Doane Robinson, Historian
Lincoln Borglum, Superintendent

EXECUTIVE OFFICES
Mount Rushmore
Keystone, South Dakota
◆

EXECUTIVE COMMITTEE
Kent Keller, Chairman
E. F. McDonald, Jr., Vice Chairman
Russell Arundel, Secretary
W. J. Bulow   William Williamson
William McReynolds, Ex-Officio

COMMITTEE ON DESIGN AND PUBLICITY
Gutzon Borglum, Chairman
W. J. Bulow   George Philip
E. F. McDonald, Jr.   Lorine J. Spoonts
William McReynolds, Ex-Officio

Dear Arthur:

Thanks for your letter, we are glad to hear from you. I know you have read that we were going on with the Hall of Records and Stairway and same time we hope to. but the government due to the defense emergency has ~~turned~~ turned down all new appropriations and we will be finished here in a month or so. Do you have any idea where Bially and I can get a job? There is not ~~enough~~ much chance of any more money here until the war is over. I am sorry to have to say this but that is the situation.

Louella is fine and we have a baby girl. Best to you and Mary. Skalla asks to be remembered to you too.

Sincerely
Lincoln

180 | LOVE Letters from MOUNT RUSHMORE

The Borglums' vision
of the Hall of Records
as a repository for the
nation's history and
treasures was never
fulfilled. However, in
1998, a small vault was
cut into the floor of
the chamber entrance.
It contains a record of
the Mount Rushmore
project. Image by
Chad Coppess. South
Dakota Department of
Tourism

With the death of Gutzon Borglum, the Mount Rushmore project was placed in the hands of his son, who was to do what might be called clean-up work. In his fall correspondence to Dad, Lincoln reported: "We have not been doing much since you left, but have now started up with a small crew." In a later correspondence, Lincoln wrote: "The government, due to the defense emergency, has turned down all new appropriations and we will be finished here in a month or so. Do you have any idea where Reilly and I can get a job?"

On October 31, 1941, "the mountain for the last time echoed the chatter of bumpers and the clamor of drills," as Rex Alan Smith put it in his book *The Carving of Mount Rushmore* (p. 398). Dad had to have realized that Gutzon Borglum's dreams for a Hall of Records and Granite Stairway had passed away for good, while Dad's own dream of returning to the Black Hills that he had come to love so deeply also vanished.

Epilogue

For the record, I have yet to find the Daughters of the American Revolution flag that I had earnestly sought for that autumn day in 2005 when I discovered the trunk of Rushmore letters, but my reward turned out to be so much greater. When I visit Mount Rushmore now and look up at that colossal monument to freedom, I see more than just the four great presidents. I see Mom and Dad. What a gift.

Mom and Dad lived long and productive lives after the events of 1939–1941. One cannot exaggerate the volume of writings that exist in the form of articles and letters pertaining to the work that my Dad, Arthur J. Cerasani, did over the thirty-some years of his life after he left Mount Rushmore. As a pioneer in the field of art therapy, Dad believed that the various forms of art could be used to aid the physical and mental health of people from all walks of life. Not limiting himself to adult education, which was being offered by the public schools, he actively sought out institutions such as sanatoriums, assisted-living facilities, nursing homes, and retirement facilities because he believed art to be

Today, tourists from all over the world visit Mount Rushmore, which boasts an impressive visitors' center and parking lot (next page) to accommodate the traffic. Images by Chad Coppess. South Dakota Department of Tourism

| LOVE LETTERS *from* MOUNT RUSHMORE

age-blind. Many leaders in the education field looked forward to having Dad involved with their programs.

In the early 1950s, Dad set up a studio in his own home so that he could serve the entire public and ensure that all could afford art instruction. I can remember meeting so many of his enthusiastic students over the years. His life could best be summed up by what his personal physician wrote at the time of his death: "There are very few Renaissance Men still around, but he certainly smacked of the genius of Leonardo da Vinci and Michelangelo in his creative drives in many fields. I was privileged to have known him and to have been his physician." My Dad, Arthur J. Cerasani, passed away on March 1, 1970, thirty years after his time on the mountain.

My mother, Mary Cerasani, had raised three of us boys—Artie, Jr., me, and my younger brother Allen. After Dad was gone, she continued to give good wisdom and advice to all who requested it. She returned to school and earned her master's degree in education, which led to her teaching positions at the Harley School

Mother joined the Peace Corps and worked in Thailand when she was seventy.

หน่วยสันติภาพสหรัฐอเมริกา (ประเทศไทย)
U.S. PEACE CORPS, BANGKOK, THAILAND.

แมรี่ เซราซานี
Mary Cerasani

Mary Cerasani
Signature

in Rochester, New York, and also in the Greece school system just outside of Rochester.

Mother never gave up her love of travel and learning. On March 22, 1980, at the age of seventy, she arrived in Thailand for training as a Peace Corps volunteer. She was assigned to a dangerous post in southern Thailand, where she taught for two years. I can vividly remember visiting her and remarking on how difficult it was to travel to the remote location where she was teaching. She insisted on living as the people of the area were living. In fact, she had none of the conveniences of home and had to endure 115-degree temperatures with no air conditioning. The legs of her table were ensconced in cups of oil to keep ants from climbing up them, and she often skirted deadly cobras as she walked to and from her classroom.

After her two-year assignment, she received a commendation letter from the United States Peace Corps, thanking her for her service. At age eighty, she re-entered the corps and was assigned to Poland to teach. She became sick while in Poland, however, and was unable to complete her assignment. My mother, Mary G. Cerasani, passed away on April 24, 2004.

Sources

INTERVIEWS

The author interviewed the following people
at various times from 2005 to 2010:

Carter, Robin Borglum (granddaughter
of Gutzon Borglum);

Cerasani, Allen and Rita (son and daughter-in-law
of Arthur and Mary Cerasani);

Cerasani, Americo (brother of Arthur Cerasani);

Fisher, Helen (sister of Arthur Cerasani);

Martin, Zane (museum specialist,
National Park Service);

Schufelt, Florence (sister of Mary Cerasani);

Williams, Robert (cousin of Mary Cerasani).

BOOKS

Borglum, Lincoln. *My Father's Mountain:
Mt. Rushmore National Memorial and How It Was
Carved.* Hermosa, S.Dak.: By the Author, 1966.

Carter, Robin Borglum. *Gutzon Borglum: His Life and
Work.* Austin, Tex.: Eakin Press, 1998.

Casey, Robert J., and Mary Borglum. *Give the Man
Room: The Story of Gutzon Borglum.* Indianapolis,
Ind.: Bobbs-Merrill Co., 1952.

Clifford, Don ("Nick"). *Mount Rushmore Q & A:
Answers to Frequently Asked Questions.* Keystone,
S.Dak.: By the Author, 2004.

Fite, Gilbert C. *Mount Rushmore.* 1952. Reprint ed.
Keystone, S.Dak.: Mount Rushmore History Assoc.,
1980.

Higbee, Paul. *Mount Rushmore's Hall of Records.* 2d
ed. Keystone, S.Dak.: Mount Rushmore History
Assoc., 2008.

Julin, Suzanne Barta. *A Marvelous Hundred Square
Miles: Black Hills Tourism, 1880–1941.* Pierre: South
Dakota State Historical Society Press, 2009.

Shaff, Howard, and Audrey Karl Shaff. *Six Wars at
a Time: The Life and Times of Gutzon Borglum,
Sculptor of Mount Rushmore.* Sioux Falls, S.Dak.:
Center for Western Studies, 1985.

Smith, Rex Alan. *The Carving of Mount Rushmore.*
New York: Abbeville Press Publishers, 1985.

Zeitner, June Culp, and Lincoln Borglum. *Borglum's
Unfinished Dream: Mount Rushmore.* Aberdeen,
S.Dak.: North Plains Press, 1976.

ARTICLES AND WEBSITES

Borglum, Lincoln. "The Hall of Records and the Great
Stairway." National Park Service. nps.gov.

Bossler, Gregory. "Horton Foote: The Bard of
Wharton." *The Dramatist* 2 (1999): 4–11.

Lubell, Samuel, and Walter Everett. "The Man Who
Carves Mountains." *Reader's Digest* (May 1940):
113–15.

"About Luigi Del Bianco." *Luigi Del Bianco:
Chief Carver on Mount Rushmore, 1933–1940.*
luigimountrushmore.com.

"Mount Rushmore." *American Experience.* pbs.org.

"Mount Rushmore National Memorial." *Experience Your America*. National Park Service. nps.gov/moru.

Perlman, David. "Four for the Ages: Gutzon Borglum Talks of His Thirteen-year Task of Carving Heroic Figures on the Side of a Mountain." *New York Times Magazine*, Aug. 25, 1940.

"The Story of Italian American Internment during WWII." Italian Historical Society of America. italianhistorical.org.

U.S. National Archives and Records Administration. archives.gov.

NEWSPAPERS

New York Times, 1939–1941.

Rochester Democrat and Chronicle, 1940–1950.

Rapid City Daily Journal, April 12, 1939.

FILMS

Zwonitzer, Mark. *Mount Rushmore.* WGBH Educational Foundation. 2001.

Index